Dallas is cooking!

by
RENIE STEVES

Nutritionist
LINDA MCDONALD, MS, RD

Foreword by
CAROLINE ROSE HUNT

FRAN FAUNTLEROY
Publisher

DALLAS IS COOKING!

Printed in the United States of America

ISBN 0-9613643-9-4

Library of Congress Cataloging-In-Publication data

Houston Gourmet Publishing Company

All recipes are reprinted with permission of authors.
Photographs printed with permission of Mark V. Davis.
LiteFare and nutritional information printed with permission of Linda McDonald.

SPECIAL THANKS TO

Mark V. Davis, Photography
Alicia Bradshaw, Editorial Assistant
Sterling W. Steves, Wine and Food Consultant
LeWay Composing Service, Inc., Design and Layout
Sprint Press, Printing
Jayroe Litho, Lithography
Avner Samuel, China
Stanley Korshak, Silverware
Ron Roberson of Bloomers, Flowers

FOREWORD

When I moved to Dallas in 1938, dining out in a restaurant was a rare occasion. Fran Langford's "Show on Ice" at the Adolphus' Century Room has eclipsed their food from my memory. The Baker Hotel's Mural Room provided me my first taste of Chicken Tettrazini, named after the opera star. I considered it much more "au courant" than the standard party fare of that time, Chicken a'la King and English peas. Every Wednesday at lunch one of the Marcus brothers commentated the Neiman Marcus style show at the hotel, from which the ladies immediately walked up Commerce Street to the store to buy what they had seen. Neiman Marcus was a tremendous influence on the fact that today Dallas is noted for the stylish chic of its ladies.

After the Saturday matinee movie at the Palace or Majestic Theaters, we usually indulged in a fabulous dessert of a cupcake topped with vanilla ice cream with hot caramel sauce served at the nearby Titche Goettinger Department Store.

The steaks served at the Golden Pheasant located on Commerce between the Adolphus and Neiman Marcus were the best in town. A stuffed Chinese golden pheasant looked down on the diners - many who came from out of the city to engage in the booming oil business.

To be assured of fresh fish, we went to Vincent's Seafood Restaurant, which was established in 1898 at 101 S. Poydras Street. They brought their fish packed in ice by truck from the Gulf of Mexico; there was no plane service in those days. Their cole slaw was wonderful. I wish I had the recipe.

El Fenix, whose original 1918 restaurant was demolished to make way for the Woodall Rogers Freeway, was the Mexican restaurant in Dallas. We always took guests from afar to sample the Mexican dishes, unknown in most of the country. Only when I visited Mexico, did I discover that El Fenix was offering Tex-Mex food, a Texas invention to later sweep the country.

At Sammy's on Greenville Avenue, I always ordered a steak sandwich with A-1 Sauce and a Dr Pepper. There was no Italian restaurant in town. We had never even heard of pizza. The Lobellos, who owned Sammy's, went on to establish the Italian Village on Oak Lawn, long a landmark eatery.

The lunches at the Sterret sisters' S & S Tea Room were deservedly popular. Willie Sterret confided that she kept a cook in the basement preparing their wonderful homemade potato chips every day. Thoughts of their sliced chicken sandwich amply covered with Thousand Island dressing still makes my mouth water. I once suggested to colorful Miss Willie that they should have a low calorie selection on their menu. "Hell," she responded. "They only say they want low calorie food, they never order it."

The S & S Tea Room did not stay open for afternoon tea. Never did I dream that one day "taking tea" would be so popular that Lady Primrose's would develop and offer a whole line of tea blends, even herbal and decaffeinated. And furthermore, that the Thatched Cottage Pantry at Lady Primrose's would be designated as offering the best tea service in the United States and be famous for scones and clotted cream as well as cottage lunches.

Today we have hundreds of restaurants to choose from, thanks to the change in the liquor laws, prosperity, and the disappearance of domestic cooks. Also many different ethnic groups have settled in Dallas bringing their distinctive types of food and the peoples to appreciate them. Dallas is famous not only for the diversity of its cuisine, but also for the creativity and quality. There are fine European-trained chefs, as well as many young American men and women chefs who are creating excellent and innovative foods. The Mansion on Turtle Creek's Dean Fearing and Routh Street Cafe's Stephan Pyles have developed Southwestern cuisine, a legitimate culinary expression which has gone far beyond the boundaries of the southwest and become a vibrant international cuisine.

This book will guide you as you explore the restaurants of Dallas for the culinary adventure, ever changing, ever exciting. Go forth and enjoy!

— CAROLINE ROSE HUNT

INTRODUCTION

Dallas Is Cooking! is dedicated to these Dallas chefs and restaurateurs who are giving their customers pleasure, excitement, comfort and delicious food and wine. It is a pleasure to showcase their restaurants and the personalities behind the action.

One of the most difficult jobs in the world is making people happy at the table. A successful restaurant is the result of challenges of expediency, of impeccable service, of acquiring fresh produce and new products, of balancing the books and of implementing new ideas and bettering old ones, for all chefs and restaurateurs. This book is about these people.

When interviewing chefs for the essays, certain themes were common throughout our conversations. Formally-trained talent reigns in Dallas. A number of our chefs, Lori Finkelman Holben, David Holben, Jim Severson, Victor Gielisse and Kevin Garvin are graduates of the Culinary Institute of America in Hyde Park, New York. Stephan Pyles, Ron Rosenbaum and Helmut Wesemann studied music, linking that artistic ability with creativity in cooking.

Simplicity in recipes and presentations is in vogue, although many chefs link several simple recipes together to create dynamic tastes. A demand for unique ingredients has created a burgeoning market for exotic foodstuffs. The increasing availability of foreign foods also preserves the integrity of the regional cuisines and cooking styles of peoples who move to Dallas and bring their cooking traditions, such as Javier Gutierrez, Lori and Efisio Farris and Annie Wong.

Caroline Rose Hunt and Vivian Young bring a traditional English tea to us, while New Orleans food is here with Kay Agnew, and a culinary trip to Central Europe may be had at Gaspar Stantic's restaurant. Rich Hollister's attitude about using the freshest ingredients creatively is typical of the caring Dallas chef.

Each restaurateur related that Dallasites want good value for their dollar. If patrons leave a restaurant hungry after what they consider an expensive meal, they will not return to that establishment again. If the wine list is intimidating and has no offerings accessible to their pocketbook, the customers will go elsewhere. Charlotte Parker and Kathy McDaniel strive to familiarize our palate with delicious wines that are affordable.

These style-making chefs have common theses in their approach to food, but their execution is diverse. A "Dallas cuisine" is emerging.

Stephan Pyles, Mario Reyes and Christian Gerber bring together discrete elements that retain the ingredient's original character. Pyles's creation of Shellfish Pan Roast with Guajillo Capellini Cakes exemplifies maintaining the natural state of ingredients in looks and taste. Nancy Beckham, Roland Schwegler and Jim Severson approach cooking in an 'a la minute' style, where ingredients are cooked separately and combined just before serving, such as salsas, pastas and grilled dishes.

Victor Gielisse, Kevin Rathbun and the Holbens combine clean layering, vibrant color, exquisitely balanced flavors and contrasting textures in a single dish. The Holben's plate of Roasted Breast of Chicken with Goat Cheese, Basil and Truffle Vinaigrette served with Risotto Cakes encompasses all of these elements. Regional boundaries are transcended as Avner Samuel, Jim Mills, Charley Sacher and Ron Rosenbaum apply the above principle to every imaginable ethnic cuisine, as in Samuel's Dancing Tasmanian Lobster with Red Thai Curry Sauce.

All of this explains the essence of Dallas cuisine at the moment . . . regional and ethnic ingredients, cooked separately to remain distinct and natural, carefully combined to achieve a blanket of vivacious flavor, contrasting texture, and brilliant color mingled in a single dish.

To address the growing interest in health and nutrition, a nutrition feature, LiteFare, has been included. Linda McDonald, M.S.,R.D., brings her special LiteFare tips, recipe modification and complete computer analysis to help you cook for your health needs and lifestyle. Look for the apple symbol to guide you to these.

We have suggested wines, in many cases both a white and a red, for most recipes as a guideline for your personal taste. A grape symbol will call your attention to these.

A book may be planned for years, but it is written only with encouragement, generosity and the support of family, friends and associates. Warmest and most affectionate personal thanks to the following people without whom I could not have survived.

Sterling Steves, my husband of 34 years, for his flexibility, humor, encouragement and friendship, and for the hours we have spent together enjoying food and wine.

Alicia Bradshaw, my extremely capable and creative editorial assistant, who discovered that getting recipes for the home cook from restaurant chefs is right up there with priorities of having your prayers answered. Without her, this book literally would not have happened.

Susie Mae Henry, my friend and housekeeper, who has been my source of sanity for over 30 years.

Mark Davis, a long-time associate and incredibly creative photographer, who perfectly captured the personalities of the chefs and restaurateurs.

LeNelle Campbell of Leway Composing, a saint of a lady, whose smile and encouragement kept me going. Heartfelt thanks to her for her perseverance and for wanting the best book possible.

David Sims, the talented artist who gave the words shape and visual texture.

My partners, Fran Fauntleroy, for allowing me to expand on her Houston Gourmet concept of a dining guide, and Linda McDonald, whose nutrition knowledge brings depth and timeliness to this book.

Danny Nowlin, the all-time nice guy at Sprint Press, whose exceptional expertise led us in the right direction.

Tony Furfari, my special friend, for his meticulous attentiveness to detail, while spending more time than most friends have proofreading this book.

Carol Bradshaw, my fitness trainer, for pushing me through weighty editing decisions.

Keith Crow, my good friend and computer programmer, who answered his phone day and night to keep the computer on track.

JoAnn Green and Erin Hill, extraordinary friends, for joining the group effort by brushing blush and adding powder where needed for the photographs.

All of these people love food and love pleasing people. We are fortunate to have such an exciting community. With our support, Dallas will continue cooking!

— RENIE STEVES

RED SNAPPER AND SALMON TARTARE
with Anchovy Butter

CARPACCIO
with Green Peppercorn Dressing

GRILLED CURRIED LEG OF VENISON
with Apricots and Tasso

ACTUELLE SUMMER SALAD

Welcome to Actuelle, and the table of Clive O'Donoghue and Chef Victor Gielisse. Actuelle's lighter, healthful cuisine smacks of fresh regional ingredients that hint of international influence. Do not look for faddish, flash-in-the-pan fare at this establishment, but for leading-edge cuisine.

The restaurant and Gielisse (pronounced hee-liss-say) have received many five-star ratings and awards. Actuelle's latest is the DiRoNA Award, as one of the Distinguished Restaurants of North America. O'Donoghue and Gielisse were honored in 1991 with the coveted Ivy Award, a prestigious hospitality industry award. Recently the restaurant was inducted into the Fine Dining Hall of Fame. Gielisse was voted America's best Seafood Chef in 1987.

Gielisse, the Culinary Institute of America 1991 Chef of the Year, predicts, "We are entering a new millennium in food technology. Chefs will have to refocus. Cooking schools are going to change their associates degree classes to a four-year program, where students will take more business, food technology, and food science classes."

In his new book, *Cuisine Actuelle*, Gielisse has combined more than 150 recipes from the restaurant with wisdom gained from his experience in the cooking profession. Emphasis is placed upon making the recipes easy for the home cook.

O'Donoghue sees changes occurring in the front of the house. "Restaurants can no longer afford to be intimidating. We are dealing with an educated consumer that expects to be made comfortable and welcome. The days of haughty service and minuscule portions are over."

O'Donoghue is a wine connoisseur, and oversees Actuelle's extensive cellar. He hosts regular wine tastings at the restaurant, and winemakers are often present to discuss their work with those attending the tastings.

Actuelle is sleek and urban in design, with a sophisticated and intimate bar separate from the multi-level dining areas overlooking the open kitchen.

───────── LITEFARE ─────────

A wide variety of starches and vegetables receive as much attention on the menu as the accompanying proteins. Look for Black Bean Soup, Stewed Leeks, Potato Cakes, Corn Pancakes, Lentil Ragout, Polenta, Orzo and Quinoa Wheat.

500 Crescent Court
Suite 165
Dallas TX 75201
214/855-0440

RED SNAPPER AND SALMON TARTARE *with Anchovy Butter*

1 9-ounce salmon fillet, skin and all bones removed
1 9-ounce red snapper fillet, skin and all bones removed
Salt to taste
Freshly ground black pepper to taste
2 tablespoons olive oil dressing (recipe follows)

ANCHOVY BUTTER
2 anchovy fillets
Pinch Hungarian sweet paprika
4 tablespoons soft butter
Freshly ground black pepper
1 tablespoon olive oil dressing (recipe follows)

OLIVE OIL DRESSING
1/2 cup extra-virgin olive oil
1/4 cup Armagnac
2 cloves garlic
12 freshly crushed black peppercorns
1 sprig fresh tarragon
1 sprig fresh lemon thyme

Cut both fillets into slices about 1/8 inch thick. Stack the slices and cut them into 1/8 inch wide strips. Cut across the strips to make 1/8 inch cubes. As you cut, discard any bones that may remain. The pieces should be small but not mushy. Place the fish in a serving bowl and season lightly with salt and pepper. Shake the olive oil dressing well and strain 2 tablespoons over the diced fish. Mix gently but thoroughly. Keep cold until ready to serve.

Anchovy Butter
Place the anchovy fillets in a bowl. With a wooden spoon, mash the anchovy fillets against the side of the bowl until they are a paste. Whisk in the paprika, butter and pepper. When the butter mixture is smooth, shake the dressing well and strain 1 tablespoon into the bowl. Whisk until smooth and thick. Chill.

Olive Oil Dressing
Place all ingredients in a jar. Shake well and let rest overnight before serving. Strain through several layers of cheesecloth before using.

To serve: Slice small baguettes of French bread into 1/4 inch slices, toast both sides and keep warm. Spread anchovy butter on toast and top with tartare. *Serves 8 as an appetizer or 4 as a main course.*

 Eliminate the Anchovy Butter and decrease fat calories to 26 percent.

 Vichon Chevrignon (California White)
Kendall Jackson Chardonnay (California White)

CARPACCIO *With Green Peppercorn Dressing*

3/4 cup olive oil
1/4 cup red wine vinegar
  2 tablespoons parsley, finely chopped
1/2 teaspoon minced garlic
  1 tablespoon chopped fresh oregano
  1 20-ounce sirloin strip

GREEN PEPPERCORN DRESSING

3/4 cup olive oil
1/2 cup parsley, chopped
1/2 cup capers, drained
1/2 cup green olives, pitted
1/2 cup Dijon mustard
1/2 cup white vinegar
1/3 cup green Madagascar peppercorns
 12 cornichons
  2 garlic cloves, chopped

In a bowl, combine olive oil, vinegar, parsley, garlic and oregano. Lay the sirloin in the marinade and turn until well coated. Marinate for four hours.

Pre-heat grill to high heat. Remove meat from marinade and pat dry with paper towels. Brown the strip very quickly on both sides then set it on a rack and place in a 500-degree oven for 3 minutes. Remove from oven and refrigerate immediately.

Once thoroughly chilled, completely trim the outside brown crust and slice sirloin into paper-thin slices.

Arrange slices on chilled plates, spoon some dressing over each portion of beef and serve with rye Melba toast. *Serves 8 as an appetizer or 4 as a main course.*

Green Peppercorn Dressing
In a food processor, blend all ingredients until just combined, 5-10 seconds.

 Serve only 1 ounce of carpaccio with 2 slices Melba toast.

 La Vielle Ferme Reserve Red (French Red)
Petit d'Noir Paso Robles (California Red)
Frescobaldi Pomino Il Benefizio (Italian White)

GRILLED CURRIED LEG OF VENISON *With Apricot & Tasso*

          2 pounds venison, from leg, cut into
             1-inch cubes
         10 ounces dried apricots
      1 1/4 cups brandy
          3 tablespoons olive oil
          3 cloves garlic, pureed
          3 large onions, sliced
          6 tablespoons smooth apricot jam
          3 tablespoons rice vinegar
          2 tablespoons brown sugar
          2 bay leaves
          2 tablespoons curry powder
          1 tablespoon salt
          1 teaspoon black pepper
          1 tablespoon lemon thyme
        1/3 cup red wine
          5 ounces tasso ham
        1/3 cup Venison stock*
          2 tablespoons butter, softened

Soak apricots in brandy to cover until plump. Heat oil in saute pan. Saute garlic and onions until translucent. Remove from heat, cool and drain on paper towels. Combine apricot jam, vinegar, sugar, bay leaves, curry powder, salt, pepper and lemon thyme. Add red wine, stir in onion and garlic and combine thoroughly.

On a wooden skewer alternate venison, apricots, and tasso ham and place in marinade. Marinate in refrigerator for at least 24 hours, turning three times.

Drain kebabs thoroughly and grill on each side for 5 minutes. Keep hot. In a separate pan, heat marinade and add 1/3 cup venison stock. Reduce the liquid, pass through a sieve, and swirl in a little soft butter. Serve sauce separately. *Serves 8.*

* Beef or veal stock are available frozen in some supermarkets, and may be substituted for venison stock.

 Venison is a very lean meat with only 14 percent fat calories. Even with the added oil in this recipe the result is just 23 percent fat calories.

ACTUELLE SUMMER SALAD

          2 pounds young green beans, washed
          1 pound white mushrooms, cut into
             julienne
          1 ounce truffles, thinly sliced
          4 tomatoes, cut in wedges
         16 artichoke hearts
             Vinaigrette (recipe follows)
          2 tablespoons minced fresh chives

VINAIGRETTE
        1/2 cup walnut oil
        1/4 cup red wine vinegar
          2 shallots, finely chopped
             Salt and freshly ground pepper

Snap off ends of beans and string them. Cook in large quantity of boiling water. Make sure that the beans remain crunchy. Cool under cold water, drain at once, and pat dry.

Place beans in a salad bowl. Top with mushroom julienne and truffle slices. Surround and alternate the tomato wedges and artichoke hearts. Season with vinaigrette and freshly minced chives. *Serves 8 as an appetizer or 4 as a main course.*

Vinaigrette - Whisk together all ingredients and toss with salad immediately before serving.

 Decrease oil to 1/8 cup to keep fat calories at 30 percent.

DANCING TASMANIAN LOBSTER
with Red Thai Curry Sauce

TIKKA SPICED CORN-FED CHICKEN
with Split Yellow Lentils and Crispy Pappadam

STEAMED GIANT SEA SCALLOPS
with Black Bean Ginger Sauce

Western meets East at Avner's on McKinney. Avner Samuel and his wife Amy have created an au courant environment to showcase his cooking talents.

Samuel's cafe-style, glass-walled restaurant decor is unique in Dallas. The black and white color scheme incorporates brightly colored carved wooden snakes from Chile to add excitement and pizazz. "Some customers like to sit near them and others don't," says Samuel. The snakes are part of Samuel's original inspiration for the restaurant.

The decision to create Avner's was made after the Samueles' trip to Hong Kong. Samuel made a trip to the art supply store for colored pencils that day and designed the logo. The snazzy logo is symbolic of the fun side of Dallas dining offered at Avner's.

"Food is like fashion; it comes and goes. I am doing more multi-ethnic type cuisine. Middle Eastern cuisine will be the next wave, since we have been through classical, American, Southwestern and Mediterranean. We are now entering eclectic," Samuel predicts.

His eclectic style is evident in his menu and wine list. Foods from around the world and from many different peoples come together on the custom-painted German china. The wine list is also a diversified collection from Third World countries, along with wines from Australia, New Zealand, South America and California.

Crispy Spiced Maple Leaf Duck With Pan-Fried Potato Pancake and Black Plum Hoisin Sauce evokes thoughts of the Orient, while Grilled Double Aussie Chops conjure a hearty appetite. The diversity of Samuel's cuisine is illustrated by his soup selections, from Singapore Tea Soup to his signature Tortilla Soup.

Samuel received his training in Israel and in France. He moved to the United States in 1980 and has worked at The Mansion on Turtle Creek and The Pyramid Room. He also worked closely with Wolfgang Puck at Toronto's Spago Festival and at Madonna's wedding.

LITEFARE

Samuel strives for a high quality, nutritious menu that incorporates lots of colorful vegetables and low-fat natural sauces. You will find very little butter or cream on this menu.

2515 McKinney Ave.
Dallas TX 75201
214/953-0426

DANCING TASMANIAN LOBSTER *with Red Thai Curry Sauce*

4 6-ounce Australian lobster tails
1 stick chopped lemon grass*
1 tablespoon chopped ginger
1/2 tablespoon minced garlic
2 tablespoons red Thai curry paste*
1 cup chicken stock
3 tablespoons butter
4 cups mixed cut vegetables
1 lotus root, peeled and thinly sliced*
1 teaspoon olive oil

Slice lobster tails into bite-size pieces and saute together with lemon grass, ginger and garlic, approximately 3 minutes until lobster is done. Add chicken stock and curry paste. Simmer until sauce is reduced by half. Add butter. Set aside.

To cook vegetables, saute approximately 4 cups mixed cut vegetables with olive oil, salt and pepper. More colorful vegetables such as snow peas, broccoli, and red and yellow bell peppers make a better presentation. Place mixed vegetables around plate, leaving space in the center for lobster. Arrange lobster in center of plate, then pour sauce over. Garnish with lotus root. *Serves 4.*

* Lemon grass, curry paste and lotus root may be purchased in Oriental markets.

 Reduce butter to 2 tablespoons.

 Jean Leon Chardonnay (Spanish White)
Chateau Souverain Chardonnay (California White)

TIKKA SPICED CORN-FED CHICKEN
with Split Yellow Lentils & Crispy Pappadam

TIKKA SPICED CHICKEN
2 corn-fed chickens,
  split in half and boned
4 tablespoons Masala spice*
4 tablespoons Tikka spice*
1 1/2 teaspoons water
1 tablespoon olive oil

LENTILS
1 tablespoon olive oil
2 tablespoons chopped bacon
2 tablespoons chopped celery
2 tablespoons chopped onion
2 cups split yellow lentils
2 tablespoons curry powder
5 cups chicken stock
  Kosher salt to taste

VEGETABLES
2 tablespoons olive oil
1 cup fennel, cut julienne
1 cup chopped broccoli
1 cup mixed bell peppers,
  cut julienne
1/2 cup corn kernels
1/2 cup baby green beans
  Kosher salt and pepper to taste
1 teaspoon chopped fresh oregano

GARNISH
4 crispy pappadam**
4 large sprigs fresh oregano

Mix all ingredients for Tikka Spiced Chicken in mixing bowl. Mix well and marinate for 24 hours. Over hot grill, cook chicken skin side down for five minutes. Turn and cook for four more minutes. Set aside.

Lentils
In a small pot place the olive oil, bacon, celery and onion. Cook over medium heat for five minutes. Add lentils, curry, and chicken stock. Bring to a boil. Add salt to taste and simmer until lentils are softened, about 20 minutes. Set aside.

In a hot skillet, crisp pappadam on both sides until color turns white. Set aside.

Vegetables
To cook vegetables, put olive oil in a saute pan, add vegetables and saute over medium heat until softened. Add salt, pepper and oregano to taste.

Place Tikka Spiced Chicken, skin side up on bottom of plate. Place lentils to left of chicken. Break pappadam in half and stand up in center of lentils. Add vegetables to right side of plate. Garnish with oregano. Serve hot. *Serves 4.*

 * Masala and Tikka spices are available in Indian markets.
** Pappadam is wafer-thin East Indian bread made with lentil flour and is available in Indian markets in various sizes and flavors.

 This is a healthy dish with an abundance of vegetables. Keep the fat low by eliminating all or some of the olive oil. Spray pan with no-stick cooking spray to saute celery, onions and vegetables; or steam the vegetables. Cook one 2 1/2-pound chicken for 4 servings to keep portion size moderate. Cook chicken with skin, but remove skin before eating.

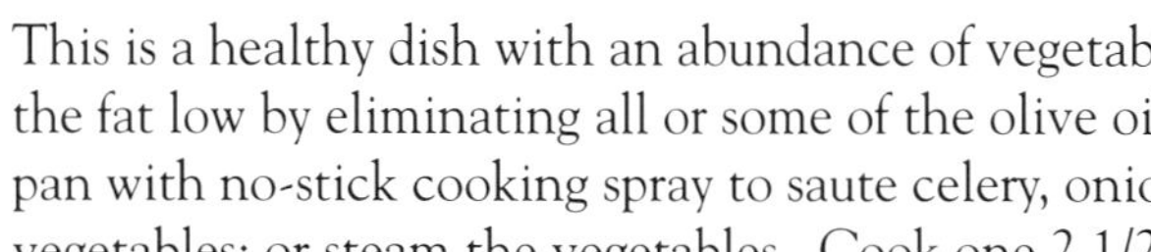 Fall Creek Sauvignon Blanc (Texas White)
Ruffino Galestro (Italian White)

STEAMED GIANT SEA SCALLOPS *with Black Bean Ginger Sauce*

20 giant sea scallops
1/4 cup chicken stock
3 tablespoons pure honey
4 tablespoons soy sauce
3 tablespoons fermented black beans*
2 tablespoons chopped ginger
4 tablespoons chopped cilantro
1 tablespoon butter
1 teaspoon olive oil
    Salt and pepper
1 cup daikon radish*
1 cup cut Japanese broccoli*
1 cup sliced carrots
1 cup baby green beans
    Cilantro leaves for garnish

Steam scallops for approximately 4 to 5 minutes and set aside. Heat chicken stock in saute pan, add honey and soy sauce. Heat until honey is dissolved. Add fermented black beans and ginger. Saute until beans are softened and slightly plumped. Add chopped cilantro and butter. Set aside.

Saute vegetables with olive oil, salt, and pepper to taste.

Place scallops in center of plate. Arrange vegetables around scallops. Pour sauce over scallops. Garnish with whole cilantro leaves. *Serves 4.*

* Daikon radish, fermented black beans and Japanese broccoli are available in Oriental markets.

Beringer Sauvignon Blanc (California White)
Cain Cellars Musque (California White)

BRAZOS TURKEY CHILI

MAIN STREET SPANISH GARLIC SOUP
with Lemon Aioli

BRAZOS ANCHO FUDGE PIE

MAIN STREET PEPPERED WALNUT FOCCACIA BUNS

Nancy Beckham's Brazos bridges Texas rivers, both the Trinity and the Rio Grande. Fort Worth-born Beckham is importing South of the Border food faster than you can say hoja santa. Her new establishment, Main Street News, offers Deep Ellum patrons a laid back place to browse through magazines and newspapers while enjoying a full meal or a piece of Warm Baci Chocolate Pie.

The food Beckham creates at Brazos is a blend of authentic Mexican, Tex-Mex and Southwestern, replete with fresh chilies. Tamales are carefully wrapped in traditional banana or hoja santa leaves (a large leaf with a mild anise flavor). Wooden desert animals, ristras, neon cactus and Navajo rugs comprise the folk art that decorates the walls.

Comfort food takes high priority. "Brazos is the type of restaurant where a guy can stop in after a long day at work, step up to the bar, loosen his tie, and say 'Bring me a King Ranch Chicken and a beer,'" says Beckham. Grilled Snapper Chalupa from the wood-burning grill or Blue Corn Chili Relleno baked in a cazuela appease any appetite.

In Beckham's style, brick walls, a black painted metal ceiling and a covered patio offer patrons comfortable places to linger and relax to live guitar music over cappucino.

Main Street News serves a different type of food from Brazos. Pear and Mustard Tart, Grilled Polenta, Smoked Virginia Trout with Brie and Almond Sandwich, and Marinated Lamb Skewers are delicious choices. Main Street also has the special desserts and brews you would expect at a coffee house and bistro.

LiteFare

Brazos: Specialty is fresh, flavorful mesquite-grilled food seasoned with Southwestern herbs and seasonings. Try the Turkey, Snapper or Vegetable Fajitas accompanied by low-fat black beans, green rice and pico de gallo.

Main Street News: Good place for couscous with grilled vegetables, turkey or chicken sandwich on freshly baked whole-grain bread. Sample the Spanish Garlic Soup, with little or no Lemon Aioli.

BRAZOS
2100 Greenville Ave.
Dallas, TX 75206
214/821-6501

MAIN STREET
NEWS
2934 Main Street
Dallas TX 75226
214/746-2934

BRAZOS TURKEY CHILI

1 large yellow onion, chopped
6 cloves garlic, minced
2 tablespoons cumin seed
6 tablespoons olive oil (divided use)
2 red bell peppers, seeded and chopped
2 poblano peppers, seeded and chopped
2 jalapeno peppers, seeded and chopped
2 serrano peppers, seeded and chopped
1 cup ancho and New Mexico Red chile paste (recipe follows)
3 tablespoons red chili powder
1 tablespoon ground coriander
1 tablespoon ground cinnamon
1 tablespoon coarsely ground black pepper
2 pounds ground turkey
4 cups chopped tomatoes with juice
2 cups chicken stock
1 cup Mexican beer
1 7-ounce can chipotle peppers in adobo sauce, coarsely chopped
1/4 cup grated unsweetened chocolate

GARNISH

Chopped green onion
Cilantro
Grated cheese
Fried tortilla strips
Sour cream

Saute onions, garlic and cumin in 3 tablespoons olive oil until transparent. Add chopped peppers and saute over medium heat about 10 minutes. Add chile paste and spices, saute 5 more minutes, set aside.

Brown ground turkey in remaining 3 tablespoons olive oil. Add tomatoes, chicken stock, beer and chipotle peppers. Simmer slowly 30 to 45 minutes.

Just before serving, stir in chocolate. Garnish with chopped green onion, cilantro, grated cheese, fried tortilla strips and sour cream. *Serves 8 to 10.*

Ancho and New Mexico Chile Paste
Remove stems and seeds from **4 ancho chilies** and **4 New Mexico red chilies**. Lightly toast chilies on a flat griddle or comal (careful not to scorch!). Cover with boiling water and let sit 10 to 15 minutes. Transfer chilies to blender and puree, adding just enough soaking liquid to make a smooth paste. Leftover paste will keep covered in refrigerator for up to one week, or frozen up to 6 weeks.

 Use ground turkey white meat and 2 tablespoons of olive oil, one tablespoon for sauteing the vegetables and one tablespoon for sauteing the turkey. Use chicken stock that is low in fat and sodium. Nutrient Analysis is without added garnishes. Green onion and cilantro are acceptable.

 Lytton Springs Zinfandel (California Red)
Hacienda Chenin Blanc (California White)
Beer

MAIN STREET SPANISH GARLIC SOUP *with Lemon Aioli*

4 tablespoons olive oil
2 large yellow onions, finely diced
1 cup minced fresh garlic
1 cup roasted garlic puree (recipe follows)
2 tablespoons dried thyme
1 tablespoon dried oregano
1 teaspoon dried tarragon
4 fresh bay leaves (or 6 dried)
2 quarts rich vegetable or chicken stock
1/2 cup dry white wine
1/2 cup sherry
   Salt and white pepper to taste
   Lemon aioli (recipe follows)
   Chopped Italian parsley for garnish

LEMON AIOLI
3 tablespoons minced garlic
4 egg yolks
3 tablespoons fresh lemon juice
1/4 teaspoon salt
2 1/2 cups olive oil

In stock pot, heat olive oil until smoking slightly. Add diced onions, garlic, garlic puree and herbs. Reduce heat and saute until onions are very soft and translucent. Add stock, bring to boil, reduce heat and simmer for 1 hour. Add wine, sherry, salt and pepper to taste.

Serve with toasted crouton topped with Lemon Aioli and chopped Italian parsley. *Makes approximately 2 quarts.*

Roasted Garlic Puree
Toss 1 cup fresh garlic cloves with 2 tablespoons olive oil. Wrap loosely in aluminum foil and roast in 350-degree oven for two hours, or until golden and soft. After garlic cools, remove from papery peel and puree in food processor.

Lemon Aioli
Combine garlic with egg yolks, lemon juice and salt in bowl of food processor. With motor running, slowly add olive oil and process until thick. *Makes approximately 3 cups.*

 This soup is fairly low in fat at 38 percent. To reduce the fat to 30 percent of calories, cut sauteeing oil to 2 tablespoons. The Lemon Aioli is very high in fat, so use in moderation.

 Kenwood Sauvignon Blanc (California White)
Far Niente Chardonnay (California White)

BRAZOS ANCHO FUDGE PIE

2 deep 9-inch pastry shells, unbaked
5 eggs
1 cup flour
1 cup sugar
1 cup packed dark brown sugar
Pinch of salt
1 pound unsalted butter, melted and cooled slightly
1/4 cup ancho chile paste (recipe follows)
24 ounces semi-sweet chocolate chips
2 cups roasted, chopped pecans
2 tablespoons vanilla extract

In a large bowl, beat eggs until thick. Sift flour, sugar, brown sugar and salt together. Beat dry ingredients into eggs until thick and smooth. Slowly beat in butter and mix well.

Fold ancho paste, chocolate chips, pecans and vanilla extract into batter. Pour batter into pastry shells. Bake at 350 degrees for 35 to 40 minutes or just until pies are set. Serve warm with fresh fruit puree or ice cream. *Makes two 9-inch pies.*

Ancho Chile Paste

Remove stems and seeds from **8 to 10 ancho chilies** and prepare as directed for chile paste in the Turkey Chili recipe.

MAIN STREET PEPPERED WALNUT FOCCACCIA BUNS

2 1/4 tablespoons active dry yeast
1 cup strong, warm coffee or espresso
3/4 cup warm water
2 tablespoons honey
5 cups all-purpose flour
2 teaspoons salt
1/2 cup chopped roasted walnuts
1/2 tablespoon coarsely ground black pepper
1 tablespoon toasted dry thyme
6 tablespoons olive oil (divided use)
1 cup stone-ground cornmeal (divided use)

Sprinkle yeast over warm coffee and warm water. Mix only until yeast dissolves. Allow to proof for 5 minutes, then stir honey through. In a large bowl, sift flour and salt. Stir walnuts, pepper and thyme through flour. Make a well in center and add yeast mixture and 4 tablespoons olive oil. Stir until well mixed. Turn dough onto table or pastry board sprinkled with cornmeal.

Knead dough until it is resilient and no longer sticky, kneading in 1/2 to 3/4 cup cornmeal to prevent sticking. Form into large ball. Place in large bowl rubbed with 1 tablespoon olive oil, rubbing top of dough with remaining olive oil as well. Cover bowl with plastic wrap and allow to rise until doubled in size, approximately 30 to 40 minutes.

Punch dough down with fist five or six times. Turn out onto cornmeal-sprinkled table and knead again for 12 good turns. Divide dough into 4-ounce sections. Roll into balls and slightly flatten into disks. Place on cornmeal-sprinkled baking sheets with enough space between buns to allow them to rise and double in size. When doubled in size, bake 8 to 10 minutes at 450 degrees until light golden. *Makes approximately one dozen 6-inch buns.*

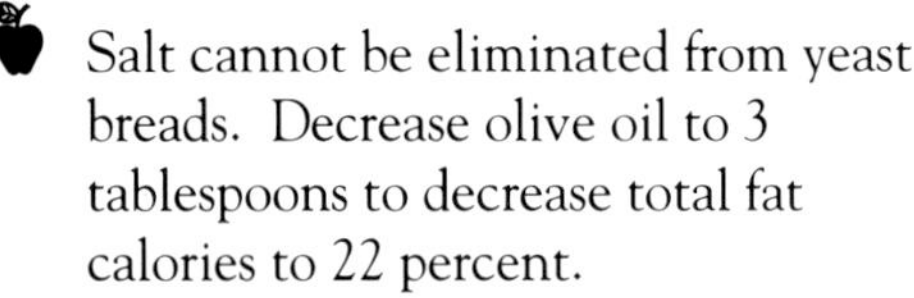 Salt cannot be eliminated from yeast breads. Decrease olive oil to 3 tablespoons to decrease total fat calories to 22 percent.

 DeLoach Zinfandel (California Red)

MARGAUX'S ALMOND CHEESECAKE
on Fresh Berry Sauce

LOUISIANA CRAWFISH AND SMOKED HAM HOCKS
over Garlic Cheese Grits

BAKED COHO SALMON ROULADES
stuffed with Gulf Shrimp & Crabmeat Dressing

Cafe Margaux transports New Orleans and Cajun cuisine to 4527 Travis. Proprietor Kay Agnew has been welcoming Dallas diners to these exciting tastes for over seven years.

The restaurant's new location on the edge of Highland Park enhances the Louisiana flavor with authentic French Quarter style and decor. The exposed brick walls, large dark wood bar, and plant-filled atrium set a Southern mood. New Orleans ambiance is heightened by live entertainment in the red brick courtyard every night. For those customers who want to learn about their future, a tarot card reader appears on Monday evenings.

Cafe Margaux invokes rich culinary tradition with authentic New Orleans entrees including a variety of fresh fish selections, and accents of French, Spanish, Cajun and Creole influence. One side of the menu is classic creole and cajun cuisine, the homestyle dishes close to the heart of regular customers. These include Crawfish Etouffee, Redfish Margaux, Fried Cornmeal Oysters with Black Pepper Cream, Gumbo, and Jambalaya. The rest of the menu holds specials of the day, which may include Grilled Fillet of Redfish, Crawfish and Shrimp Enchiladas with Queso, Grilled Cajun Ribeye, and generous sandwiches and salads at lunch.

Agnew is among the Dallas restaurateurs who insist upon the freshest foodstuffs. Even pasta is homemade daily at Cafe Margaux. Although Agnew was in the catering business for seven years before opening the restaurant, she says, "People don't know I can cook." Agnew continues to cater for a variety of music groups and television and commercial shoots. "My favorite caterings are cocktail buffets," she says. "I don't want to get into white glove dinners."

Cafe Margaux's private dining room is a big draw. Agnew says, "Our executive clientele say they think more creatively in a neutral place."

Agnew has served as a beverage consultant for Dallas charity events such as TACA and the Beaux Arts Ball. She is particularly knowledgeable about good value and wine selection, and has done her homework on the excellent wine list at Cafe Margaux.

"I like chatting with my customers and making people feel special," she says of Cafe Margaux. "One asset is that we are small, with only 90 seats, and can nurture a friendly atmosphere."

LITEFARE

Cajun cuisine starts with a roux made from butter and flour. Although beans, rice and seafood are added, the resulting dishes are usually high in fat. Order the grilled fish, with the sauce on the side, or Cold Cajun Boiled Shrimp with lemon and Creole cocktail sauce.

4527 Travis
Dallas, TX 75205
214/520-1985

MARGAUX'S ALMOND CHEESECAKE *on Fresh Berry Sauce*

CRUST
1 1/2 cups graham cracker crumbs
2 tablespoons sugar
1 teaspoon flour
1/4 cup melted butter

FILLING
2 pounds cream cheese, room temperature
1 cup sugar
2 eggs, beaten
1/2 teaspoon vanilla
1/2 teaspoon almond extract

TOPPING
1 pint sour cream
3/4 cup sugar
3/4 teaspoon almond extract
1/2 teaspoon fresh lemon juice

FRESH BERRY SAUCE
2 pints fresh strawberries, raspberries or blueberries, washed and stemmed
1 cup sugar

Crust
Combine ingredients. Press into bottom of an 8-inch springform pan and halfway up the sides. Bake at 350 degrees for 5 minutes and cool.

Filling
Combine ingredients and mix until smooth. Pour into prepared crust and spread evenly. Place in cold oven, turn oven to 350 degrees and bake for 30 minutes.

Topping
Pour fresh berry sauce on top of baked cheesecake. Spread evenly and bake at 350 degrees for 8 minutes. Cool, then regrigerate for 1 hour before serving. Slice and place on pool of fresh berry sauce. *Serves 10 to 12.*

Fresh Berry Sauce
Puree berries and sugar in blender or food processor, strain and serve.

 Moet & Chandon White Star Champagne (French Champagne)
Roederer Estate Brut (California Sparkling)

LOUISIANA CRAWFISH AND SMOKED HAM HOCKS
over Garlic Cheese Grits

1/4 cup chopped yellow onion
1/4 cup chopped green bell pepper
2 teaspoons minced garlic
1 1/2 cups heavy cream
    Pinch basil
    Pinch cayenne pepper
1/2 pound crawfish tails, cooked and peeled
1 cup cooked ham hock meat, diced
    Salt and pepper
2 cups garlic cheese grits (recipe follows)
2 tablespoons chopped green onion

GARLIC CHEESE GRITS

1/2 cup chopped onion
1 teaspoon vegetable oil
    Pinch of cayenne pepper or hot sauce to taste
1 teaspoon garlic powder
3 cups water or clear chicken stock
1/4 teaspoon salt
3/4 cup quick grits
1 cup Monterey Jack cheese
1 egg, beaten
    Parmesan cheese for garnish

Saute onion, pepper and garlic. Add cream, basil and cayenne. Reduce to sauce consistency. Stir in crawfish and ham hocks. Season to taste with salt and pepper. Arrange a small portion of grits on plate and spoon mixture alongside. Garnish with chopped green onion. *Serves 8 as an appetizer or 4 as a main course.*

Garlic Cheese Grits

Saute onion in vegetable oil until transparent. Sprinkle with cayenne and garlic powder. Add water or chicken stock and salt and bring to a boil. Add grits and return to boil. Turn heat down and simmer for 5 minutes. Set aside.

Add cheese and egg. Whip into grits. Bake at 350 degrees for 20 to 30 minutes. Sprinkle top with Parmesan before baking if desired.

 The Garlic Cheese Grits are lower in fat if you substitute low-fat Monterey Jack for regular cheese.

 Bonny Doon Clos de Gilroy (California Red)
Hogue Cellars Chardonnay (Washington White)

BAKED COHO SALMON ROULADES
Stuffed with Gulf Shrimp & Crabmeat

  2 whole Coho salmon fillets
1/2 medium onion, diced
1/2 green pepper, diced
  1 tablespoon extra-virgin olive oil
  6 ounces gulf shrimp, diced
  2 cups small croutons
    Pinch cayenne
    Pinch oregano
    Pinch thyme
  1 tomato, diced
  3 ounces lump crabmeat
1/2 cup fish stock
1/2 cup bread crumbs
    Salt and white pepper to taste
    Lemon butter for garnish

Saute onion and pepper in oil until translucent. Add shrimp, croutons and seasonings and cook for 5 minutes. Add remaining ingredients.

Spread dressing onto fillet, leaving skin on if you desire. Roll fillets and secure with a toothpick. Place in oiled baking pan, seam side down. Bake 10 to 15 minutes at 400 degrees. Pass lemon butter separately. *Serves 8.*

 Saute onion and pepper in a non-stick pan with cooking spray and omit the lemon butter. Cut fillet into 3 1/2 to 4-ounce servings.

 DeLoach Sauvignon Blanc (California White)
Emilio Lustau Solera Reserva "Jarana" Fino (Spanish Dry Sherry)

CAFE PACIFIC CIOPPINO
PATRIZIO LINGUINI VERDE
CAFE PACIFIC FRAISES AU POIVRE NOIR
CAFE PACIFIC WHITE CHOCOLATE MOUSSE
SHRIMP PACIFIC

Cafe Pacific and Patrizio are members of the same Dallas restaurant family, and sit face to face in Highland Park Village. When asked the secret of owning two successful restaurants, owner Jack Knox replies that great reporting systems keep him in close touch with daily performance. "I have been accused all of my life of having a fanatical attention to detail," says Knox.

"My favorite thing about this business is the customer. The customer always knows if a restaurant is honest with them in food, service, and value. My least favorite thing is an occasional food critic who thinks he or she knows more than the 500 or 600 customers who vote for a place with their presence every night."

Knox has enjoyed great success with Cafe Pacific for many years. "We celebrate Cafe Pacific's anniversary in September each year. This year it's number twelve, and it looks like a record year," says Knox.

In developing the Italian restaurant concept for Patrizio, Knox asked himself, "Where would I like to spend my Italian dining dollar?" The answer was any one of Rome's big 'Italian food halls.' Knox has recreated that atmosphere so he no longer has to leave Dallas to satisfy his desire.

Authentic eighteenth-century art hangs on Patrizio's Mediterranean, buttery-colored walls, surrounding an upbeat atmosphere. Its focused menu and impressive wine list are priced to please the value connoisseur. The restaurant has become a very popular local watering hole, and neighborhood action revolves around the bar on Thursday evenings and weekends.

Roland Schwegler, chef at Patrizio, says, "I am sticking with the trend of lighter food. Pasta dishes are 75-percent of our customers's orders." Knox considers Schwegler the "quintessential professional."

CAFE PACIFIC
24 Highland Park Village
Dallas TX 75205
214/526-1170

PATRIZIO
25 Highland Park Village
Dallas TX 75205
214/522-7878

LITEFARE

Cafe Pacific: Try the Pommery Salad or Hearts of Palm and Asparagus Salad with vinaigrette dressings on the side. Order Sesame Seared Scallops or the Grilled Vegetable Plate, and Angel Hair Pasta and Tomato Sauce as an entree.

Patrizio: Look for low-fat sauces: marinara, tomato, clam. Best choices are Capelli d'Angelo with Marinara Sauce, Linguini with Clam Sauce, and the Vegetable Pizza.

CIOPPINO

3/4 cup olive oil
1 cup sliced onions
3/4 cup diced celery
3/4 teaspoon crushed garlic
3/4 pound tomatoes, peeled, seeded
and diced
2 teaspoons tomato puree
1 tablespoon chopped fresh parsley
1 tablespoon chopped green onion
1 tablespoon chopped green pepper
1/4 teaspoon oregano
1/8 teaspoon cayenne pepper
1/2 teaspoon salt
1/4 teaspoon freshly ground black
pepper
8 hard-shell clams, washed
1/2 pound crab claws, shelled
1/2 pound raw shrimp, peeled and
deveined
3/4 pound boneless raw cod or sea bass
fillet, cut into 2-inch pieces
1 1/4 cups dry white wine
1 cup fish stock (if unavailable,
substitute clam juice)
1 lobster tail* (optional)

Heat olive oil in a heavy pot. Add onions, celery and garlic; simmer briefly. Add tomatoes, tomato puree, parsley, green onion, green pepper and all remaining seasonings, except white wine and fish stock. Cook over low heat for 30 minutes.

Add all raw fish and shellfish along with white wine and fish stock. Cook, uncovered, slowly for 20 minutes (any pre-cooked seafood should be added only during the last 5 minutes of cooking). Do not stir while simmering. *Serves 4.*

* For a richer, more flavorful preparation, add 1 lobster tail, cut into 1-inch pieces.

 Cut olive oil to 2 tablespoons and reduce fat to 30 percent of calories. Eliminate the olive oil, and the fat is only 9 percent of calories.

 Frog's Leap Sauvignon Blanc (California White)
Saintsbury Carneros Pinot Noir (California Red)

LINGUINI VERDE

12 ounces spinach linguini
4 tablespoons olive oil
1/4 teaspoon minced garlic
4 ounces mushrooms, sliced
1/2 cup sun-dried tomatoes, cut julienne
1/4 cup pine nuts, toasted
Pinch of salt and pepper
1/2 cup chicken stock
6 tablespoons unsalted butter

Cook pasta and set aside. In a hot saute pan, combine olive oil, garlic, mushrooms, sun-dried tomato and pine nuts. Toss lightly. Add seasoning, then chicken stock and butter. When mushrooms are slightly tender (about 2 minutes) add pasta, toss well and serve. *Serves 2 as an entree or 4 as a side dish.*

 Eliminate the butter, decrease olive oil to 2 tablespoons, and pine nuts to 1 tablespoon. Fat calories drop to 35 percent.

 Monsanto Chianti Classico Riserva (Italian Red)
Chateau Gloria (French Red)

FRAISES AU POIVRE NOIR

2 pints strawberries, cleaned and halved
Granulated sugar to taste
5 teaspoons brandy
2 tablespoons plus 1 teaspoon Grand Marnier
1 teaspoon whole black peppercorns, cracked*

Put strawberries in a bowl and sprinkle with sugar. Add brandy, Grand Marnier and cracked pepper. Let berries marinate 15 minutes, and serve in individual bowls. *Serves 4.*

* Crack whole peppercorns on cutting board with a heavy object or in a mortar. DO NOT use a peppermill, as the grind will be too fine.

 Good healthy dessert. Only 5 percent fat calories.

 Bonny Doon Framboise (California dessert wine)
Taittinger Brut La Francaise (French Champagne)

WHITE CHOCOLATE MOUSSE

8 ounces white chocolate
2 cups whipping cream
1/2 cup sugar
3 egg yolks
1 whole egg
2 tablespoons plus 1 teaspoon water
1/4 teaspoon vanilla extract
1 teaspoon kirsch*

Melt chocolate in a pan over boiling water. Whip cream until stiff and refrigerate for later use. Put sugar into heavy saucepan with water. Boil until cooked to syrup stage.

Beat eggs in mixing bowl for 2 minutes. Slowly pour in sugar syrup while beating. Remove bowl from machine and add melted chocolate with rubber spatula. Let cool. Next, slowly fold in whipped cream, vanilla, and kirsch. Refrigerate 4 hours before serving. *Serves 8.*

* Kirsch is a clear cherry brandy.

SHRIMP PACIFIC

6 tablespoons unsalted butter (divided use)
1 pound medium shrimp, peeled and deveined
4 shallots, finely chopped
4 broccoli florets, steamed
8 mushrooms, sliced
1/2 zucchini, cut julienne
1 teaspoon Spices Seascape (recipe follows)
1/2 cup dry white wine
2 cups heavy cream
1/4 cup chopped fresh parsley
Salt

In a heavy skillet, melt 3 tablespoons butter and saute the shrimp, shallots, broccoli, mushrooms and Spices Seascape for one minute. Deglaze the pan with white wine and add the cream. When the shrimp have turned pink (approximately 2 to 3 minutes), take them from the pan and reserve them so as to avoid overcooking. Reduce the pan liquids by half. Add the rest of the butter in small pieces and stir to blend in the butter. Add the chopped parsley. By this time, the sauce should be thick. Adjust the seasonings to taste.

Arrange the shrimp on a serving plate and cover with sauce. *Serves 4.*

Spices Seascape:
1 teaspoon cumin, 1/2 teaspoon cayenne pepper, 1 teaspoon gumbo file, 1 teaspoon paprika, 1/4 teaspoon celery salt, 1 teaspoon sage, 1/2 teaspoon nutmeg, 1/2 teaspoon saffron, 1 1/2 teaspoons curry powder and 1 teaspoon coriander.

Grgich Hills Sauvignon Blanc (California White)
Sonoma-Cutrer Russian River Chardonnay (California White)

ORIENTAL GLAZED ROAST QUAIL

POTATO-GREEN CHILE SOUP

GRILLED PORK LOIN
with Jalapeno Barbecue Sauce

GRILLED LAMB CHOPS PROVENÇAL

Food is a family affair at City Cafe. Join Mardi Schma, her children, and Chef Richard Hollister in the casual ambiance of this neighborhood cafe serving Regional American food, with wines from an award-winning list.

Chef Hollister exercises culinary creativity with an ever-changing array of meals produced in the open kitchen. On-the-job training in Dallas preceded his move to City Cafe four years ago. Hollister incorporates international flavors in Florida Grouper with Black Beans, Lime and Plantains, his Greek version of Roasted Rack of Lamb topped with Onions, Calamata Olives, Feta and Lemon, and Alsatian Warm Cabbage Salad.

"Rich is very creative," says Schma. "He loves seafood and changes the menu every week." Hollister meets this challenge with meals which emphasize seasonal bounty such as Grilled and Skewered Salmon and Scallops, Pan-Seared Veal Tenderloin with Three Mustard Caper Sauce, or Grilled Mexican Redfish with Spicy Tomatillo Butter.

The restaurant is warm and inviting to friends, families and faraway travelers. A large dining room upstairs accommodates a variety of private gatherings. Schma, managing partner, says her favorite part of the business is "exciting people about food."

Choose a Chocolate Toffee Torte or Blueberry Meringue Cake and relax with a remarkable selection of brandies, ports and dessert wines to top off any meal.

City Cafe added City Cafe To Go two years ago. Here delicious foods are prepared for eating on the spot or for carry-out.

The Schma (pronounced Smay) siblings shoulder many of the responsibilities of the restaurants. Daughter Katie is chef and manager of City Cafe To Go, Jennifer handles bookkeeping for both restaurants, son Doug is the pastry chef of City Cafe, Peter is in training for a restaurant job, and Sarah works part-time at both restaurants while attending school.

LITEFARE

Waiters will assist you in making light choices. Menu states that special requests are welcome and items can be prepared for specific tastes or dietary needs.

5757 West Lovers Lane
Dallas, TX 75209
214/351-2233

ORIENTAL GLAZED ROAST QUAIL

8 semi-boneless quail
1 pound Oriental noodles

MARINADE
1/2 cup honey
1/4 cup maple syrup
6 tablespoons lime juice
1/4 cup chopped scallions
1 teaspoon Oriental chili paste
1/2 teaspoon salt

SAUCE
4 tablespoons lime juice
1 cup chicken stock
Reserved marinade
2 tablespoons sesame seeds, toasted
1/2 bunch cilantro, chopped

Combine all marinade ingredients and marinate quail overnight. Strain and reserve marinade. In a deep skillet, over medium-high heat, sear quail 4 to 5 minutes per side.

Remove to serving platter. Deglaze pan with lime juice, add stock and reserved marinade. Reduce by half. Stir in sesame seeds and cilantro.

Cook noodles and arrange on plate. Add two quail and spoon sauce over. *Serves 4.*

 Quail, like most fowl is a lean meat with most of the fat in the skin. Cook the quail with the skin on to keep the meat moist, but remove the skin before eating. This reduces the fat calories from 58 percent to 32 percent. The marinade and sauce are very low in fat and sodium.

 Schramsberg Blanc de Blancs (California Sparkling)
Reserve St. Martin (French Red)

POTATO-GREEN CHILE SOUP

1 tablespoon vegetable oil
6 roasted Anaheim chilies, peeled, seeded, chopped
1 medium onion, finely diced
2 teaspoons minced garlic
1 teaspoon toasted cumin seed
1 jalapeno, seeded and diced
1/4 cup gold tequila
1/4 cup lime juice
1 teaspoon black pepper
6 cups chicken stock (preferably homemade)
3 large Idaho potatoes, peeled and diced
Salt
1/2 bunch cilantro, chopped

Heat oil in a large pot. Add the next five ingredients. Saute over medium heat 5 minutes. Add tequila and cook 2 minutes. Add lime juice, pepper, stock, and potatoes and bring to a boil. Simmer until potatoes are cooked. Salt to taste. Garnish bowls with chopped cilantro, ladle the soup over cilantro and serve. *Serves 6.*

 Delicious low-fat soup. Use defatted chicken stock.

 Domaine Ott Bandol Rose (French Blush)
Trefethen Chardonnay (California White)

GRILLED PORK LOIN *with Jalapeno Barbecue Sauce*

3 pounds boneless pork loin, trimmed and sliced into 1/2-inch thick medallions
1 large red onion
5 fresh jalapeno peppers
4 tablespoons canola oil
1 cup orange juice
1 ounce Grand Marnier
3 ounces Worcestershire sauce
2 quarts ketchup
4 tablespoons rice vinegar
2 seedless oranges peeled and segmented
2 tablespoons brown sugar
1 teaspoon dry mustard

Puree onion and jalapenos together. Heat oil in pan over medium high. Saute onion and jalapeno for 6 minutes. Add orange juice and Grand Marnier, reducing by two thirds. Stir in remaining ingredients. Lower heat to a light simmer and cook 1 1/2 hours, stirring occasionally.

Heat grill until coals are white. Lightly oil the grates. Place medallions on grill for 2 minutes, basting the top sides with barbecue sauce. Turn over and cook the other side 2 minutes, and baste. Turn 45 degrees and flip them over again; baste and cook one minute. Turn over again. You should have beautiful cross-marks from the grill. Cook 1 to 2 minutes more, then serve. *Serves 6.*

 Pork loin is a low-fat meat, but cut amount to 2 pounds for 6 servings. This gives a 5-ounce portion per person, which stays below the American Heart Association recommendation of less than 6 ounces per day. The barbecue sauce is low in fat and sodium and would be good for other meats. Since this recipe makes approximately 3 quarts, you will have plenty for other uses.

 DuBoeuf Beaujolais (Regnie or Brouilly) (French Red)
Antinori Orvieto (Italian White)

GRILLED LAMB CHOPS PROVENÇAL

16 lamb chops, trimmed
 1 cup extra-virgin olive oil
1/4 cup good Cabernet Sauvignon
 4 anchovies, chopped
 4 teaspoons minced garlic
1/4 cup parsley, chopped
 1 tablespoon chopped fresh basil
 1 tablespoon chopped fresh rosemary
 1 tablespoon chopped fresh thyme
 1 teaspoon salt
   Freshly cracked pepper
 2 ripe tomatoes, chopped

Mix together all ingredients except chops. Coat lamb chops with the marinade and refrigerate overnight. Pre-heat grill. When flame has subsided from grill, drain the lamb, reserving marinade for basting. Lamb chops should be grilled twice on each side for approximately two minutes for medium rare, depending on thickness. Baste lightly and try to avoid getting oil in the fire.

Serve with a crisp salad and rosemary roasted new potatoes. *Serves 4 to 6.*

 Lamb is a high fat meat, so look for chops with little visible fat. Veal chops (32 percent fat calories) could be substituted for lamb chops (75 percent fat calories). Cut portion from 4 to 2 lamb chops per person. This will give about 4 ounces of lamb per person. Serve with a low-fat salad and starch to balance the extra fat in the lamb. The marinade is high fat, so use sparingly.

 Sterling Three Palms Vineyard Cabernet Sauvignon (California Red)
Chateau Larose-Trintaudon (French Red)

BRAZOS
Tangi Beckham
owner's
Chef

CONSERVATORY and BEAU NASH

GRILLED FLORIDA GROUPER
with Avocado-Orange Sauce, Herb Salad and Crisp Rice Fritters

CHESAPEAKE OYSTER STEW
with Beaten Biscuits

TORTILLA SALAD
with Black Bean Cakes & Jalapeno Ranch Dressing

Hotel Crescent Court beckons hungry travelers and locals alike to its elegant eateries, The Conservatory and Beau Nash. These distinctive restaurants share a kitchen directed by talented Executive Chef Jim Mills, formerly chef de cuisine at The Mansion on Turtle Creek.

The Conservatory
HOTEL CRESCENT COURT

Experience the outdoors inside at The Conservatory. A 20-foot-high glass wall makes the long narrow room feel elegant and open.

Mills's healthful style is the refreshing result of his open attitude to the staff's experiments and suggestions. Executive Sous Chef Roger Kaplan says, "We love to try new things. Jim may decide to grab a handful of a new grain and throw it in the deep fryer just to see what it does."

"I love what I do," says Mills. "What we do should make people happy." His philosophy matches the commitment to service at the Hotel Crescent Court. "Taking care of customers and making them feel special," is a very important goal, says Mills. "This happens in the dining room and on the plate."

The Conservatory menu presents a classic American array of the chef's imaginative interpretations of House Smoked Salmon on Six Grain Croutons, Peppered Rabbit and Artichoke Ragout with Marjoram Noodles, and Coriander Cured Rack of Lamb with Wild Mushroom Scalloped Potatoes. Seafood is a predominant item, and delectable desserts top it all off.

Beau Nash delivers both fun and serious food within its high-ceiling domain. The dark wood bar stands alone in attracting a dynamic crowd of Dallasites and travelers to the bistro atmosphere. Regulars can dine at Beau Nash six nights running and never eat in the same country. The menu spans the globe from Texas T-Bone to Greek Salad to Curried Vegetable Dumplings to Tortilla Crusted Catfish to Jerked Chicken With Mango Black Bean Relish and Tomato-Coconut Sauce.

LITEFARE

The Conservatory: The cream sauces on the menu are thickened with cornstarch and then finished with cream. Try the Herb Oil Grilled Swordfish with Steamed Vegetables and Roasted Shallot Vinegar.

Beau Nash: Try the special items "Nutritionally balanced by The Spa at The Crescent." One of these recipes is included, Tortilla Salad with Black Bean Cakes.

Hotel Cresent Court
2200 Cedar Springs
Dallas TX 75201
214/871-3200

GRILLED FLORIDA GROUPER
with Avocado-Orange Sauce, Herb Salad and Crisp Rice Fritters

4 7-ounce black grouper fillets
2 tablespoons canola oil
  Salt and freshly ground black pepper
1 avocado, cut into 1/4-inch dice
1/2 red bell pepper, thinly julienned

ORANGE VINAIGRETTE
2 tablespoons orange juice
2 tablespoons champagne vinegar
1 teaspoon finely grated orange zest
3 tablespoons canola oil
1 teaspoon finely minced shallot
1/2 teaspoon finely minced garlic
1/2 teaspoon salt
1/4 teaspoon black pepper

HERB SALAD
1/4 cup mizuna leaves*
8 sprigs Italian parsley, remove stems
2 sprigs each fresh dill, basil, thyme, tarragon and mint
1/2 small zucchini, cut into julienne
1/4 cup french green beans (haricot vert), blanched
1/2 carrot, peeled, julienned & blanched
1/2 orange, peeled and cut into sections
1/2 lime, peeled and cut into sections

CRISP RICE FRITTERS
1 cup rice flour
1/2 cup all-purpose flour
1 teaspoon baking powder
1 egg, beaten
1/2 cup milk
  Dash salt
1 cup cooked rice

Let coals burn down under grill until ashen. Rub fillets with oil and season with salt and pepper. Lightly oil grill surface. Place fish on grill, laying fillets at a 45-degree angle to grill rods. After one minute, reposition at 90 degrees to original angle. After 40 seconds, turn and continue to cook until interior flesh becomes opaque rather than translucent. Remove from grill when cooked and transfer to a heated plate. Keep covered and warm.

To assemble, drizzle 1 tablespoon of the vinaigrette around each of four warmed service plates. Sprinkle with avocado dice and red bell pepper julienne. Place a fillet in the center of each plate and garnish with a bit of the salad tossed with some crisp rice fritters. Serve immediately. *Serves 4.*

Orange Vinaigrette
Whisk together all ingredients. *Makes 1/2 cup.*

Herb Salad
Strip stems from herbs and coarsely chop. Combine all ingredients in a large mixing bowl and toss with 1/3 cup orange vinaigrette.

* Mizuna is an adapted Asian salad herb available at some specialty markets. Substitite chicory or frisee if desired.

Rice Fritters
In a small mixing bowl combine rice flour, all-purpose flour, baking powder, egg, milk and salt. Stir gently until just combined to form thick batter. Place rice in another mixing bowl. Add just enough batter to allow grains to adhere to form a ball. Spoon by 1/2 teaspoons into oil heated to 350 degrees and fry, turning, until golden. Drain on paper towels and serve immediately. Makes 1 1/2 cups of batter, about 72 fritters.

 Eliminate the oil on the fish and the rice fritters to reduce the fat in this recipe to 38 percent of total calories.

 Gauer Estate Vineyard Chardonnay (California White)
Adler Fels Sauvignon Blanc (California White)

CHESAPEAKE OYSTER STEW *with Beaten Biscuits*

2 teaspoons canola or other light oil
2 slices pancetta bacon, chopped, blanched 30 seconds, drained
1 clove garlic, minced
1/2 onion, diced
1 rib celery, diced
20 oysters, shucked, liquor reserved
1 medium potato, peeled, diced, and blanched 1 minute
1/4 cup small lima beans, cooked
3 cups half-and-half
1 cup chicken stock
1 teaspoon Old Bay Seafood Seasoning
Cracked black pepper
Salt
Juice of 1/2 lemon
Dash of Worcestershire sauce
6 sprigs parsley, chopped, for garnish
1/2 red bell pepper, cut into very small dice, for garnish

20 Beaten Biscuits (recipe follows)

BEATEN BISCUITS
2 cups flour
1 teaspoon salt
1/4 cup vegetable shortening
4 tablespoons butter
1/2 cup ice water

Add oil to large saucepan and heat. Add pancetta, garlic, onion, and celery. Cook until fat is rendered and pancetta is crisp, about one minute. Add oysters and cook until plumped. Remove oysters with slotted spoon to a warm bowl and keep warm. Add potato, beans, half-and-half, and chicken stock. Bring quickly to a boil. Then reduce heat and add Old Bay, black pepper and salt. Let boil one minute until slightly thickened. Then add lemon juice and Worcestershire. Correct seasoning. Divide oysters among four heated soup plates, then ladle stew over the oysters. Sprinkle top of servings with parsley and red bell pepper. Place 5 beaten biscuits on stew in a circle and serve immediately. *Serves 4.*

Beaten Biscuits
Mix flour and salt. Cut in shortening and butter. Add water very slowly and work in mixing bowl 20 minutes. If using a food processor, process 2 minutes with dough blade. Dough should appear elastic and shiny. Roll out very thin, then fold over on itself. Prick well, cut out in 3/4-inch rounds and bake at 350 degrees until puffed, brown, and crisp like a cracker.

 Substitute whole milk for half-and-half.

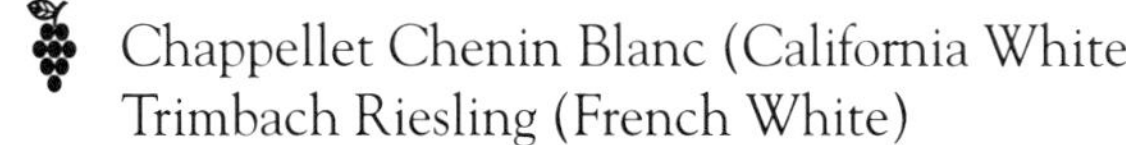 Chappellet Chenin Blanc (California White)
Trimbach Riesling (French White)

TORTILLA SALAD *with Black Bean Cakes & Jalapeno Ranch Dressing*

Salad Mix of radicchio, red oak, frisee, bibb, watercress

12 black bean cakes, silver dollar-size (recipe follows)

4 corn tortillas, cut into julienne and fried crisp

1 cup julienne of carrot, zucchini and yellow squash

1 cup prepared guacamole

1 cup Seven Sprout Mix (available at Whole Foods Market)

8 ounces jalapeno ranch dressing (recipe follows)

1/2 cup cherry tomatoes, cut in half

12 fried tortillas, cut into long triangular spikes for garnish

BEAN CAKES

1/2 tablespoon vegetable oil

1/2 yellow onion, chopped

1 cup black turtle beans

1 quart cold chicken stock

1/4 teaspoon cumin

1 tablespoon cilantro

2 tablespoons ancho chile paste (recipe follows)

1/4 teaspoon cayenne pepper

1 teaspoon minced garlic

Salt and pepper

JALAPENO RANCH DRESSING

1/2 cup sour cream

3 cloves garlic

1 jalapeno

1 bunch cilantro

1/2 cup buttermilk

2 tablespoons chopped fresh herbs

Salt and pepper to taste

Saute, in a small amount of oil, black bean cakes two minutes on each side and keep warm. In a bowl place salad mix, julienned tortillas, vegetables and tomatoes and toss with ranch dressing. Place equal amounts of salad on four plates, place three bean cakes around the salad, and top salad with equal amounts of guacamole and sprouts. Into the bean cakes stick the tortilla spikes straight up for garnish. *Serves 4.*

Bean Cakes

In a small saucepan heat oil, add onion and saute until translucent. Add beans and chicken stock. Bring to a boil then reduce to simmer. Cook beans until tender but firm, about one hour. Once beans have cooked, drain, let stand 20 minutes. Place all ingredients in a food processor. Turn on approximately 10 seconds, scrape sides and repeat two more times. Mixture should be lumpy. Season with salt and pepper. Form into silver dollar-size cakes.

Ancho Paste

2 ancho chilies, stem and seeds removed

Place washed chilies in 1 cup water in a small saucepan. Bring to a boil over medium-high heat, then reduce heat to a simmer for 10 minutes. Remove from heat and let stand 20 minutes. Pour mixture into a blender and carefully puree. Paste should be smooth. *Makes about 1/2 cup.*

Jalapeno Ranch Dressing

Combine all ingredients in a blender or food processor. Blend until smooth. Season with salt and pepper. *Makes one cup.*

 Omit guacamole and bake the tortilla chips to reduce fat to 25 percent of total calories

 Clos Du Bois Merlot (California Red)
Fetzer Gewurztraminer (California White)
Meeker Zinfandel (California Red)

GRILLED CHICKEN BREAST
with a Five Bean Chili Sauce

WHOLE-WHEAT ANGEL HAIR PASTA
with Shiitake Mushrooms and Crabmeat

CROOKNECK SQUASH AND TOMATO SOUP

PEAR CAKE
with Cream Cheese Icing

CRAB CAKES

TORTILLA SOUP

Lincoln Center is home to Crockett's, where Doubletree Hotel Executive Chef Charlie Sacher exhibits his expertise with cuisine from many lands. "Learning is constant," Sacher says. "You are always being challenged by something new."

Sacher's classical training and experience are a strong base for these new ideas. "The food served at Crockett's is traditional in this region, such as blackened tenderloin, yet has an international flair from the many different countries I have worked in," says Sacher. Daily specials demonstrate his use of interesting combinations such as Fresh Steamed Amberjack with Roast Red Pepper and Sweet Papaya Relish, and Pan-seared Glazed Duck Breast with Apple and Raspberry Custard.

"Every time you write a menu, the customers' desires are uppermost in your mind," Sacher says. "Today one of those desires is healthful cuisine."

In addition to fish and meats, Crockett's menu offers great homemade pastas. The waiters suggest these to health-conscious customers. "We have a machine that can make many shapes of pasta," says Sacher. "We price pasta dishes reasonably and offer a large assortment of sauces and accompaniments."

Sacher likes to cook with wine and herbs. "A hearty game dish goes well with thyme and Cabernet Sauvignon, lamb with rosemary and Zinfandel, and fish with basil and Chardonnay," he says. Sweet wines or liqueurs such as Chambord and Grand Marnier are used in desserts.

Sacher says, "The recipes I have written for *Dallas Is Cooking!* are quite simple and easy for the home cook. Karl Brandmeir, Food and Beverage Director of the hotel says, "We've taken a new direction in Crockett's. We are making the atmosphere more fun instead of stuffy. Our waiters now wear wild ties and button-down oxford cloth shirts." The 110-seat restaurant has a European feel condusive to relaxing conversation or a business meeting. "It was a men's club atmosphere, but it's now toned down to a bistro-style restaurant,"says Brandmeir.

Lincoln Center
5410 LBJ Freeway
at Dallas Tollway
Dallas, TX 75240
214/934-8400

─────── LITEFARE ───────

Special requests for dietary needs are welcome here. Have pasta with a low-fat tomato sauce or sauteed vegetables.

GRILLED CHICKEN BREAST *with a Five Bean Chile Sauce*

6 6-ounce boneless, skinless chicken breasts
1 tablespoon finely chopped fresh herb mixture
1 teaspoon chopped jalapeno
Salt and pepper to taste
1 clove garlic
1 tablespoon chopped onion
1 teaspoon olive oil
1 cup Five Bean Soup mixture, uncooked
1/2 cup tomato puree
1 teaspoon chili powder
Dash cumin
1 cup tomato juice
1/4 cup chopped cilantro

Marinate chicken breasts with herbs, jalapeno, salt and pepper for at least 45 minutes. In a skillet saute onions and garlic in olive oil. Add the five bean mixture with as much water as called for on the package, and all other ingredients and let it simmer for about 45 minutes or until beans are tender.

Grill chicken breasts over hot coals until they are done. Slice chicken on the bias. Spoon bean mixture onto plate and fan chicken breast over the beans. *Serves 6.*

 Chateau Ste. Michelle Chardonnay (Washington White)
Simi Chenin Blanc (California White)

WHOLE-WHEAT ANGEL HAIR PASTA
with Shiitake Mushrooms and Crabmeat

12 ounces fresh whole-wheat angel hair pasta
2 tablespoons olive oil (divided use)
6 ounces sliced shiitake mushrooms
6 ounces lump crabmeat
3/4 cup light sour cream
Salt and pepper
1 teaspoon tarragon
2 whole red bell peppers, roasted, skin removed and pureed
1 cup diced red, yellow, and green bell peppers, mixed

Cook whole-wheat pasta in plenty of salted boiling water for 3 minutes, drain, and toss with 1 tablespoon olive oil. Saute mushrooms in remaining olive oil for 3 minutes. Add crabmeat, sour cream, seasoning, and red pepper puree.

Arrange pasta in center of plate. Top with crab and mushroom sauce. Garnish plate with diced bell peppers. *Serves 6.*

 Healthy, low fat dish. Omit salt from the pasta water.

 Etude Pinot Noir (California Red)
Il Poggione Brunello di Montalcino (Italian Red)

CROOKNECK SQUASH AND TOMATO SOUP

1 tablespoon vegetable oil
1 leek, white part only, thinly sliced
1 pound crookneck squash,
   thinly sliced
1/2 teaspoon oregano
1 teaspoon fresh summer savory
   or 1/2 teaspoon dried savory
5 cups chicken stock
2 large ripe tomatoes, seeded and
   coarsely chopped
4 sun-dried tomatoes, cut into strips
2 medium potatoes, diced
   Salt and pepper

In a 4-quart saucepan heat vegetable oil and saute leeks until tender. Add squash, oregano, and savory and cook for another 3 minutes. Add stock, bring to a boil, add tomatoes and potatoes. Reduce to a simmer, cover and cook for 10 minutes. Add salt and pepper to taste. *Serves 6.*

Scharffenberger Brut (California Sparkling)
Bigi Orvieto Classico Secco (Italian White)

PEAR CAKE *with Cream Cheese Icing*

2/3 cup brown sugar
1 cup vegetable oil
   Pinch of baking powder
   Pinch baking soda
   Pinch cinnamon
1/4 teaspoon ginger
1/4 teaspoon salt
1 3/4 cups all-purpose flour
6 eggs
1 1/2 pounds pears
   Butter and flour for pan

CREAM CHEESE ICING
1/2 pound cream cheese
1 pound powdered sugar
3 tablespoons lemon juice
2 teaspoons vanilla

Preheat oven to 350 degrees. Grease and flour (may use no-stick cooking spray) a 10-inch cake pan. Mix together brown sugar, vegetable oil, baking powder, baking soda, cinnamon, ginger, salt and flour and beat on medium speed for 5 minutes. Add eggs slowly.

Peel, core and cut pears into 1-inch chunks. Fold into batter. Pour into pan. Bake for 45-50 minutes.
Serves 12.

Cream Cheese Icing
Allow cream cheese to soften at room temperature. Beat ingredients together and spread on cooled cake.

Chateau Lafaurie-Peyraguey Sauternes (French dessert wine)

CRAB CAKES

1 pound lump crabmeat
2 green onions
1/2 cup corn kernels
1/4 cup red bell pepper, diced
1/4 cup green bell pepper, diced
1 tablespoon whole grain mustard
1 egg yolk
1/4 cup bread crumbs
Dash cayenne pepper
1/2 cup flour
1/2 cup olive oil

Remove any cartilage and bone from crabmeat. Mix all ingredients well and shape into 16 2-ounce crab cakes. Dredge in flour and saute in hot olive oil until golden brown on both sides.

Serve with mayonnaise seasoned with cayenne pepper. *Serves 8.*

 Alexander Valley Vineyards Chardonnay (California White)
Rochioli Sauvignon Blanc (California White)

TORTILLA SOUP

1 tablespoon vegetable oil
1 onion, coarsely chopped
2 garlic cloves
8 tomatoes, chopped
2 ribs celery, chopped
1 mild green poblano chile, seeded and chopped
1 jalapeno chile, seeded
6 corn tortillas
2 quarts tomato juice
2 quarts chicken stock
Salt and pepper
Pinch of oregano
Pinch of cilantro
Pinch of cumin
Pinch of chili powder

GARNISH
Diced avocado, diced grilled chicken, shredded cheddar, fried julienne tortillas

Saute onion in oil until lightly brown. Add tomatoes and celery, saute for 5 minutes. Add chilies. Cut tortillas in quarters and add. Add tomato juice and chicken stock and let simmer for 2 1/2 hours. Add all spices and puree. Strain, adjust seasonings and garnish with 1 tablespoon of each of the above. *Serves 12.*

 This soup is low-fat, but watch the add-ons. Avocado, cheese and fried tortilla chips are all high fat. Best choice is the grilled chicken.

 Mumm Cuvee Napa (California Sparkling)
Gruet Blanc de Noir (New Mexico Sparkling)

SPICY PEANUT SAUCE

DAKOTA'S CAESAR DRESSING

VENISON SAUSAGE QUESADILLAS

TOASTED PUMPKIN SEED SALSA

BANANA NUT RAVIOLI
With Vanilla Bean Sauce

CRAB CAKES

Venture into the canopied elevator that stands alone at 600 N. Akard and descend to Dakota's, a chic subterranean restaurant established in 1984. Shimmering walls of water fall from street level to the patio, cutting off the bustling city above. At this downtown haven Corporate Executive Chef James Severson lifts New American grill cooking to sophisticated heights.

Dakota's relaxed atmosphere permeates its elegant decor. Gas-fed wall sconces, art deco chandeliers, slow ceiling fans and old-fashioned tavern chairs complement the polished brass, beveled glass and Italian marble floor. The indoor-outdoor dining environment has an enormous courtyard with trees, plantings and an open-air mesquite grill.

The restaurant's grill credo is reflected in the list of appetizers from Grilled Artichokes to Grilled Chicken Relleno. The kitchen's wood-burning grills offer a choice of mesquite, hickory, and fruitwood flavors.

"Grilling and skillet cooking allow me to use two tools, contrast and simple presentation. Using the freshest ingredients is the first step to building contrast in a dish through color, texture, flavor and temperature," says Severson. His menus incorporate fish, meats and game into popular regional dishes. Vibrant sauces and imaginative accompaniments of local foodstuffs surround generous portions of entrees.

When asked what the customers want today, Severson replies, "Hefty portions of hearty food that have good value. We work on things that don't cost the guest an arm and a leg. Our plates might have one-half of a lobster with something else rather than serving a two-pound lobster."

Severson is the Culinary Institute of America 1986 valedictorian. He may pursue a teaching career, to share his knowledge with young chefs in a learning environment; and like most chefs, he would like to open his own restaurant at some point in the future.

LITEFARE

"Light Fare" items on the menu list calories, fat and cholesterol. The fat calories are held at or below 20 percent, with smaller servings of chicken or fish and larger servings of carbohydrates. The Fruit Plate With Grilled Mango Puree is a special dessert.

600 North Akard St.
Dallas TX 75201
214/740-4001

SPICY PEANUT SAUCE

1/2 cup peanut oil
1/2 cup diced onion
10 dried red chile peppers
1 clove garlic, minced
1/2 cup smooth peanut butter
3/4 cup Coco Lopez
1 tablespoon chopped fresh cilantro
1/2 cup water
2 cups smoke-flavored barbecue sauce

Heat oil in pot until smoking. Add onions and peppers, cooking until translucent; then add garlic, peanut butter and Coco Lopez. Remove from heat and stir. Put in blender with cilantro and water and blend. Add barbecue sauce, strain and cool. *Makes one quart.*

Serve this sauce with shrimp, chicken, vegetables, and pork.

 Coco Lopez, a canned coconut milk concentrate is very high in saturated fat. With the peanut butter and peanut oil, there is a lot of fat in this sauce. Use in moderation.

 Trimback Gewurztraminer (French White)
Berlucchi Cuvee Imperial Brut (Italian Sparkling)

DAKOTA'S CAESAR DRESSING

2 1/2 ounces anchovies, chopped
(approximately 3 tablespoons)
1 1/2 teaspoons garlic, minced
2 teaspoons Dijon mustard
1/4 cup red wine vinegar
1 tablespoon lemon juice
1 tablespoon Worcestershire sauce
1/4 cup shredded Parmesan cheese
2 teaspoons cracked black pepper
1 teaspoon salt
3 egg yolks
1 1/2 cups olive oil
2 cups safflower oil

In food processor or blender puree anchovies, garlic, mustard, vinegar, lemon juice, Worcestershire, Parmesan, pepper and salt into a paste. Remove anchovy paste and set aside in a small bowl.

Rinse food processor or blender. Blend egg yolks and slowly add oil until it begins to thicken. Incorporate all the oil to form base. Slowly add anchovy paste until blended. Taste for seasoning. Cover and let sit overnight in refrigerator for best flavor.

Adjust seasonings, and toss romaine lettuce and croutons with some dressing. *Makes approximately 4 1/2 cups.*

 Callaway White Riesling (California White)
Cambria Chardonnay (California White)

VENISON SAUSAGE QUESADILLAS

8 flour tortillas, 6 to 8 inches
8 ounces Monterey Jack cheese, shredded
6 ounces venison sausage, cut into small dice
1/2 bunch cilantro, chopped
1 small jalapeno, seeded and minced
1/4 cup vegetable oil
Salt and pepper to taste

On one tortilla place approximately 2 ounces cheese, 1 1/2 ounces of sausage, a sprinkle of cilantro and minced jalapeno to taste. Cover with another tortilla and place into moderately hot skillet with enough oil just to cover bottom. Brown one side (spinning periodically) then flip and brown other side. Cut into 6 or 8 wedges and serve. *Serves 4.*

Try these additional quesadilla ideas: Crab, Spinach & Monterey Jack Cheese; Shredded Pork, Raisins and Ancho-Chile Cheese; Goat Cheese, Leeks & Smoked Salmon; Sharp Cheddar, Broccoli & Scallions; Pesto, Tomato and Fresh Mozzarella Cheese; Fontina Cheese, Proscuitto & Sage.

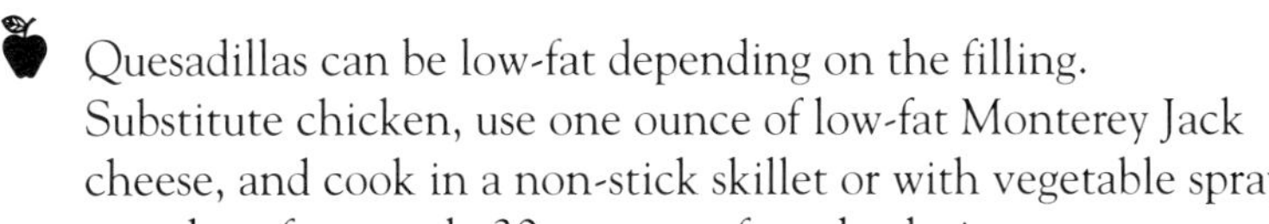 Quesadillas can be low-fat depending on the filling. Substitute chicken, use one ounce of low-fat Monterey Jack cheese, and cook in a non-stick skillet or with vegetable spray to reduce fat to only 30 percent of total calories.

 Mondavi Pinot Noir (California Red)
Niebaum-Coppola Rubicon (California Red)

TOASTED PUMPKIN SEED SALSA

6 large ripe tomatoes
1 medium onion, cut into large dice
1 medium poblano, peeled and seeded
1 tablespoon olive oil
2 garlic cloves
1 small jalapeno, seeded
Vegetable oil
1/2 bunch cilantro
1 tablespoon lime juice
1/2 cup pumpkin seeds, toasted
2 teaspoons cumin
1 tablespoon salt
2 teaspoons black pepper

Toss first three ingredients in bowl with oil just to coat. Grill until charred slightly. Return to bowl, and add remaining ingredients. Mix in food processor to a rough consistency. Serve warm. *Makes one quart.*

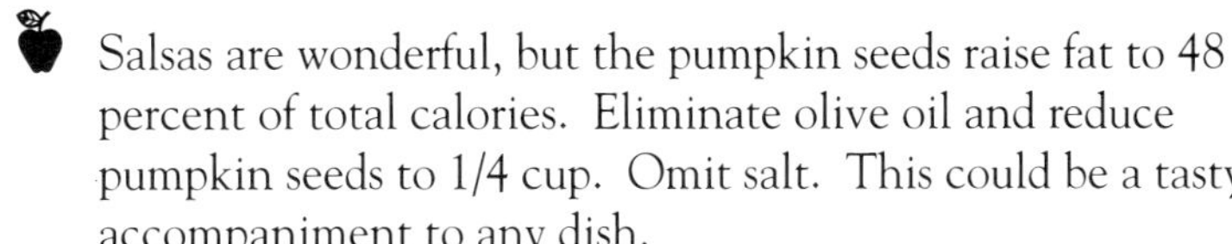 Salsas are wonderful, but the pumpkin seeds raise fat to 48 percent of total calories. Eliminate olive oil and reduce pumpkin seeds to 1/4 cup. Omit salt. This could be a tasty accompaniment to any dish.

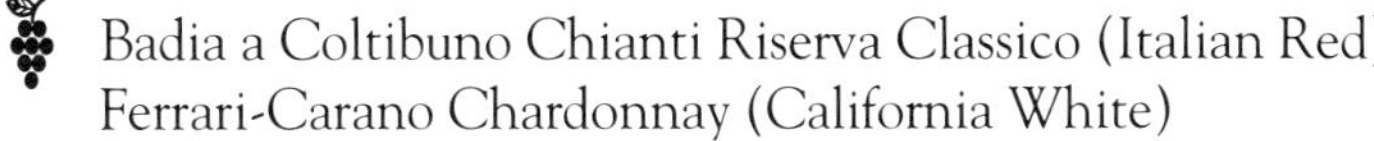 Badia a Coltibuno Chianti Riserva Classico (Italian Red)
Ferrari-Carano Chardonnay (California White)

BANANA NUT RAVIOLI *with Vanilla Bean Sauce*

RAVIOLI
 3/4 **cup diced banana**
 1/4 **cup brown sugar, firmly packed**
 1/4 **cup graham cracker crumbs**
 1/8 **cup walnut pieces**
 1/8 **cup pecan pieces**
 2 **tablespoons egg wash**
 12 **square wonton wrappers (3x3-inch)**

VANILLA BEAN SAUCE
 2 **cups heavy cream**
 1 **egg yolk**
 1/4 **cup sugar**
 1 **teaspoon vanilla**
 Seeds from 1 vanilla bean

Combine banana, brown sugar, graham cracker crumbs and nuts. Mix until moist. Egg wash 4 sides of wonton then put one teaspoon of banana filling in the center of each. Fold one time, corner to corner to form a triangle, and press both sides. Deep fry until golden brown. Serve warm. *Serves 4.*

Vanilla Bean Sauce
In a stainless steel bowl, combine cream, egg yolk and sugar. Set over boiling water and stir frequently until thick enough to coat back of spoon. Add vanilla and vanilla bean seeds. Keep warm and serve 1/4 cup portions.

 Ferrari-Carano 1989 Late Harvest Sauvignon Blanc "Eldorado Gold" (California dessert wine)
Chateau Doisy Daene (French dessert wine)

CRAB CAKES

 6 **ounces jumbo lump crabmeat, cleaned**
 1/4 **teaspoon serrano chile pepper, seeds removed, finely minced**
 1 **tablespoon celery, finely diced**
 1/2 **tablespoon purple onion, finely diced**
 2 **tablespoons crushed saltine crackers**
 1 **tablespoon mayonnaise**
 1 **teaspoon lemon juice**
 Salt and pepper to taste
 1/4 **teaspoon olive oil**

In a bowl, mix together crab, minced serrano, diced celery, diced onion, crushed crackers, mayonnaise, lemon juice, salt and pepper. Divide into 4 equal portions and press into 4 patties.

Heat heavy skillet over medium heat, add olive oil and crab cakes. Saute both sides until golden brown. Serve with lemon wedges and tartar sauce. *Serves 4.*

 Substitute low-fat mayonnaise and use cooking spray to saute the cakes.

 Morgan Chardonnay (California White)
Signorello Semillon (California White)

LOBSTER SALAD
with Sweet Mangoes

CROWNED CENTER CUT PORK LOIN
with a Cranberry Glaze

PAN-FRIED BRUSSELS SPROUTS
with Roasted Shallots and Applewood Smoked Bacon

Executive Chef Kevin Garvin presides over the hallowed halls of The French Room at the famed Adolphus Hotel, the distinguished culinary cornerstone of Dallas.

Garvin's masterful execution of nouvelle and classic haute cuisine matches the opulence of The French Room. His stellar presentations glitter under crystal chandeliers and ceiling murals in the main dining room. Recent refurbishing of the room heralds Garvin's evolution to more innovative, Neo-classic cuisine, which he describes as, "lots of classical dishes made new by adding modern ingredients, fresh herbs, and flavored oils."

When asked about his cooking technique, the 1978 Culinary Institute of America graduate says, "I like to infuse flavors by marinating, or reducing stock, or with emulsions made in a blender." Lasagna of Shrimp and Scallops with Spinach and Saffron and Chive Beurre Blanc graces the menu, as well as Crayfish and Crabmeat Salad with Curry Mayonnaise and Red Pepper Oil.

Chef Garvin chronicles the culinary evolution of his cooking in his new book, *Seasoned in Texas: The Adolphus Cookbook*. Here he presents each dish in the context of a seasonal celebration or famous event.

The French Room
AT THE ADOLPHUS

Garvin says of the Dallas cuisine scene, "It's settled now, there are not a lot of new flash-in-the-pan places. The best restaurants have claimed their places and have gathered a strong following. Trends are being dictated by our guests' needs and wants. The word for the 90's is THRIFTY. People want and expect lower prices and bargains."

An elegant three-course tea is served in the hotel lobby, which reflects the French Room decor. Guests may nibble on finger sandwiches, scones, truffles and pastries while listening to classical piano music.

In 1912, St. Louis beer baron Adolphus Busch created the French Room as the crown jewel of his namesake Dallas hotel. Dinner guests may relax before the fireplace in The French Room Bar among beautiful 17th, 18th and 19th century antiques before dinner.

LITEFARE

Garvin calls his new menu Neo-classic, the new French cuisine that eliminates butter and cream, and uses vegetable stocks, purees and emulsions to carry flavors. Portions are substantial, and each plate is balanced with vegetables and starches.

The Adolphus Hotel
1321 Commerce Street
Dallas, Texas 75202
214/742-8200

LOBSTER SALAD WITH SWEET MANGOES

4 one-pound lobsters
1 tablespoon olive oil
3 cloves garlic, peeled and crushed
2 shallots, peeled and chopped
1 serrano chile pepper, seeded
1 cup white wine
2 cups chicken stock (optional)
1 cup mango puree
1 teaspoon chopped cilantro
1 teaspoon chopped basil
2 fresh mangoes, peeled and diced
2 ounces field greens salad, cleaned
  Mint vinaigrette (recipe follows)
1 tomato, peeled, seeded and diced

MINT VINAIGRETTE

  Juice of 1/2 lemon
1/4 cup olive oil
1 teaspoon chopped fresh mint
  Salt and pepper

In a pot of salted water, place live lobsters and cook for 6 to 7 minutes. Then shock them in ice water. Remove meat from shells and dice into 1-inch pieces. Reserve meat and shells.

Heat olive oil in a heavy saucepan over medium heat. Add lobster shells, garlic, shallots and serrano pepper. Sweat without coloration, then pour in white wine and reduce until almost dry. Add chicken stock, mango puree, cilantro and basil. Bring to a boil and simmer for 30 minutes. Strain through a colander and reserve liquid. Discard shells.

Put strained liquid into a saucepan and return to heat. Add diced mangoes and cook until mango dice are soft. Puree sauce in blender and strain. Refrigerate.

To serve, pour mango sauce on each dinner plate. Toss field greens and lobster with vinaigrette and arrange in center of plate. Garnish with diced tomatoes. *Serves 4.*

Mint Vinaigrette
Combine all ingredients and whip vigorously. Season to taste.

 Sweat lobster shells, garlic, shallots and pepper in wine rather than olive oil and reduce this recipe to 33 percent fat from calories.

 Merryvale Meritage (California White)
Cuvaison Chardonnay (California White)

CROWNED CENTER CUT PORK LOIN *with a Cranberry Glaze*

1 8-inch pork loin with chin bone removed and ribs shortened and finished
3/4 cup olive oil (divided use)
4 sprigs of rosemary
1 cup cranberries
2 ribs of celery, chopped
1 large onion, chopped
1 whole leek, chopped
3 carrots, chopped
4 cloves garlic, minced
10 shallots, chopped
2 cups cranberry juice
Salt and pepper to taste

SAUCE

2 cups red wine
2 cups chicken stock
5 sprigs parsley
8 peppercorns
1 clove

Rub the pork loin with 1/4 cup of the olive oil, rosemary, salt, and pepper. Heat another 1/4 cup of oil in a roasting pan in a 450-degree preheated oven. Place pork loin, meat side down, in a pan and brown completely before turning over. Remove from the pan and cover with aluminum foil. Place the cranberries, celery, onions, leek, carrots, garlic and shallots in the pan and put meat on top. Reduce oven temperature to 350 degrees.

Mix together 1/4 cup of oil and cranberry juice. Use this to baste the loin. Roast the loin for approximately 1 1/2 hours or until internal temperature reaches 150 degrees. Remove loin from the pan and allow to rest 45 minutes before slicing. *Serves 6.*

Sauce

Remove any grease from the pan and place pan over medium heat. Pour red wine into the pan and bring to a simmer. Using a wooden spoon, deglaze the pan by scraping the vegetables that have adhered to the bottom. Reduce wine by one half. Add chicken stock and the rest of the ingredients. Reduce again by one half. Strain through a fine sieve or leave vegetables in sauce and serve.

 Use a trimmed pork tenderloin and limit portion to 5 ounces per person. Remove all grease from pan before making sauce.

 McDowell Valley Grenache (California Blush)
Carneros Creek Pinot Noir (California Red)

PAN-FRIED BRUSSELS SPROUTS
with Roasted Shallots and Applewood Smoked Bacon

2 1/2 cups medium brussels sprouts
4 cups chicken stock
2 cups small shallots, cleaned and peeled
1 cup applewood smoked bacon, diced

Soak and rinse brussels sprouts very well and cut in half. Place brussels sprouts in a 2-quart saucepan and cover with chicken stock. Bring to a simmer and cook the sprouts al dente; refresh with cold water, drain well and cool completely. In a saute pan, slowly pan fry the shallots on low to medium heat for about 15 minutes. Add the bacon. Continue cooking until the bacon is crisp. Drain the shallots and bacon, reserving the fat.

In a saute pan, heat one tablespoon of the reserved fat from the shallots and bacon. Saute the sprouts to a light golden color. Add the shallots and bacon, and serve. *Serves 6.*

 Cut bacon to 1/2 cup and use just 1/2 tablespoon of the bacon fat for sauteeing sprouts.

 Glen Ellen Gamay Beaujolais Proprietors Reserve (California Red)
Chateau Montelena Chardonnay (California White)

FACING PAGE from left: Kevin Garvin, The French Room; Charley Sacher, Crockett's; James Severson, Dakota's; Jim Mills, The Conservatory and Beau Nash

FOLLOWING PAGE from left: Gaspar Stantic, Gaspar's; Kathy McDaniel, Charlotte Parker, The Grape

Kevin P. [...]
Executive C[hef]
CHARLIE PALMER
EXECUTIVE CHEF
Dakota's
Executive Chef
Jim Severson
Jim Mills
Executive Chef
Hotel Crescent Court

POTATO CRUSTED BLACK SEA BASS
with Creamed Leek and Lobster Compote and Cabernet Sauce

BEEF TENDERLOIN
with Herb Crust and Cabernet Sauce

SHRIMP
with Carrot Juice and Thai Spices

ADRIATIC SHRIMP SOUP

Gaspar and Debra Stantic have a secret. They have a five-star restaurant in Coppell. Gaspar's amazes diners with Stantic's award-winning Alpine cuisine, an authentic combination of Swiss, German, and Austrian dishes.

Join the Stantics for dinner in a restaurant as comfortable as your home. The cozy atmosphere inside is similar to a rural restaurant tucked into a valley in the Alps. An open kitchen overlooks the 85-seat dining room decorated with Texas antiques, such as a pump organ and buffet hutches. Flowers twirl on a trellis overhead.

Stantic's international background is evident in the menu. "We would be hung in effigy if we removed certain dishes our regular customers are fond of," says Chef Steve Pilat. "Lobster and Crayfish Napoleon, 'Adriatic Style' Shrimp Soup and Rigatoni Pasta with Italian Sausages, Roasted Peppers, Mushrooms, Smoked Bacon and Romano Cheese in Spicy Marinara have been on the menu since I came over a year ago," he says.

Stantic's cuisine is prepared in the traditional European style. Rich sauces such as Fresh Rosemary Cream, Peppercorn and Horseradish Butter grace the pasta, meats and seafood which abound on the menu.

Gaspar's is top-ranked among chic Dallas restaurants, epitomizing the city's international fare. An exceptionally experienced chef, Stantic is French and Austrian-trained, and has worked for 29 years in countries as diverse as Germany, Holland, Japan, Hong Kong, Egypt, Kuwait and the United States. He has won 26 top prizes at culinary competitions.

Stantic says, "You don't build a house from the roof. Use simple fresh food, nothing complicated, and build your menu using knowledge of the culinary classics. This is basic."

LITEFARE

Gaspar's menu states, "We will be happy to adapt the menu to meet your health priorities." All sauces are made to order. A grilled vegetable plate is available with rice or pasta.

150 South Denton Tap Road
Coppell TX 75019
214/393-5152

POTATO CRUSTED BLACK SEA BASS
with Creamed Leek and Lobster Compote and Cabernet Sauvignon Sauce

2 6-ounce black bass fillets or
  4 3-ounce fillets
32 paper-thin slices of peeled potato
  Egg wash
  Fresh mint for garnish

COMPOTE

3 cups leeks, cut into 1/4-inch dice
1 cup lobster meat, cooked,
  cut into medium dice
1/4 cup chopped shallot
1/4 cup diced red bell pepper
1/4 cup diced yellow bell pepper
1/4 cup finely diced tomato
1 cup heavy cream
2 tablespoons butter
  Salt and pepper

SAUCE

1 cup Cabernet Sauvignon
4 teaspoons chopped shallots
1 1/2 tablespoons butter

Bass fillets
Wrap each fillet with slices of potato and seal with egg wash. Saute seam side down, 4 minutes each side.

Compote
Saute leek, lobster, shallot, peppers and tomato for 2 minutes. Add cream and reduce by half. Finish with 2 tablespoons butter. Season to taste.

Sauce
Reduce wine by half in saucepan. Add shallots and butter to finish.

Presentation
Place leek compote in center of plate 1/2 to 1/4-inch from rim. Place fillet of top of compote and drizzle Cabernet Sauvignon sauce over leeks. Garnish with fresh mint. *Serves 4.*

 Eliminate the butter and substitute half-and-half for the cream.

 Matanzas Creek Merlot (California Red)
Flora Springs Cellar Select Cabernet Sauvignon (California Red)

BEEF TENDERLOIN *with Herb Crust and Cabernet Sauce*

HERB CRUST

2 1/4 cups fresh egg-bread breadcrumbs
2 cups chopped fresh parsley
3 tablespoons chopped fresh thyme, or 2 teaspoons dried
1/2 cup (1 stick) unsalted butter, melted
Salt and pepper

SAUCE

2 bottles Cabernet Sauvignon
1 bottle tawny Port
4 cups beef stock or canned unsalted broth*

BEEF & POTATOES

4 medium baking potatoes
3/4 cup whipping cream
4 tablespoons olive oil (divided use)
Salt and pepper
Ground nutmeg
4 1-inch thick beef tenderloin steaks (about 8 ounces each)
1/4 cup unsalted butter

Herb crust
Combine breadcrumbs with parsley and thyme. Pour butter over, season with salt and pepper, and mix well.

Sauce
Pour red wine, Port and stock into heavy large pot. Bring to simmer over medium-high heat. Continue to simmer until reduced to 1 cup, about 1 hour and 45 minutes. (Can be prepared 2 days ahead. Cover sauce and crust mixture separately and refrigerate.)

Beef and potatoes
Bring a large saucepan of salted water to boil. Add potatoes and cook until tender. Drain potatoes and return to pan. Cook over low heat until dry, about 3 minutes. Peel warm potatoes; press through ricer into bowl. Using electric mixer, add cream and 2 tablespoons oil and beat until potatoes are smooth. Season with salt and nutmeg. Place potatoes in pastry bag fitted with 3/8-inch (No. 8) plain tip.

Season steaks with salt and pepper. Heat remaining 2 tablespoons oil in heavy large skillet over high heat. Brown steaks about 4 minutes per side.

Preheat broiler. Spread breadcrumb mixture on top of steaks, pressing to help coat. Broil until breadcrumbs are golden brown. Place steaks on a bed of pureed potatoes piped through a pastry bag into center of plate. Heat sauce in medium saucepan. Whisk in butter. Nap steaks with sauce and serve. *Serves 4.*

* Chicken and veal stock is available in the freezer section of many supermarkets.

 To lower the fat in this entree, cut portion of beef to 6 ounces per person; saute beef in a non-stick pan; use 1/4 cup margarine for crust; substitute 3/4 cup skim milk and 1/3 cup nonfat dry milk for cream; eliminate olive oil from the potatoes and butter from the sauce.

 Iron Horse Cabernet Sauvignon (California Red)
Groth Cabernet Sauvignon (California Red)

SHRIMP *with Carrot Juice and Thai Spices*

1 cup diced carrots
2 cups bottled carrot juice
2 tablespoons finely chopped lemon
   grass or lemon zest
2 tablespoons fresh lime juice
1 teaspoon finely chopped lime zest
1 small red chile, minced, or dried
   crushed red pepper
24 medium uncooked shrimp, shelled
   and deveined
2 tablespoons chopped fresh cilantro
2 tablespoons chopped fresh mint
3 tablespoons butter
   Fresh mint sprigs

Bring small saucepan of water to boil. Add carrots and cook 4 minutes. Refresh in cold water and drain. Transfer carrots to large saucepan. Add carrot juice, lemon grass, lime juice, lime peel and red chile. Bring to boil. Add shrimp; simmer until pink and opaque, about 3 minutes. Finish with butter. Ladle into bowls and garnish with mint sprigs. *Serves 4.*

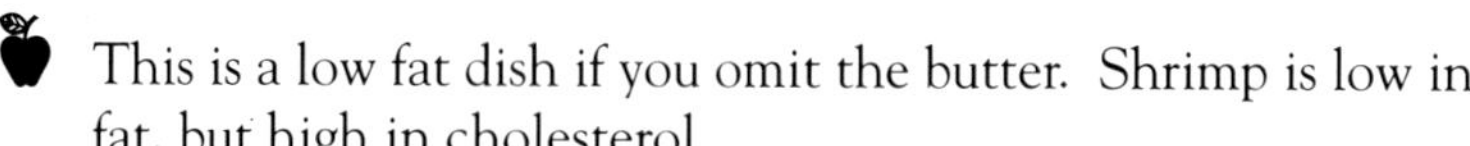 This is a low fat dish if you omit the butter. Shrimp is low in fat, but high in cholesterol.

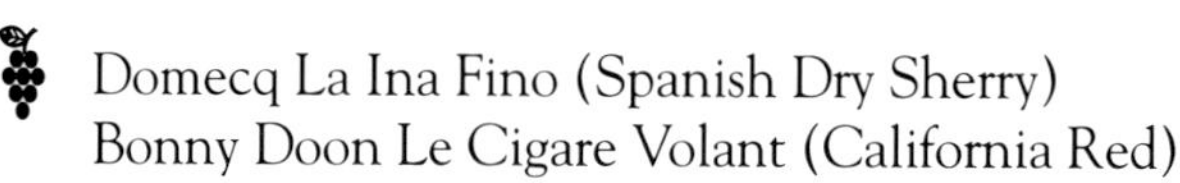 Domecq La Ina Fino (Spanish Dry Sherry)
Bonny Doon Le Cigare Volant (California Red)

ADRIATIC SHRIMP SOUP

1 tablespoon olive oil
1 tablespoon bacon, diced
1/4 cup finely diced red peppers
1/4 cup finely diced yellow pepper
1/4 cup finely diced jalapenos
1/4 cup chopped onions
1 teaspoon minced garlic
1 cup tiny raw shrimp (60-70
   count), peeled
1 1/2 cups chicken stock
1 1/2 cups marinara sauce or canned
   chopped tomatoes

Saute bacon in olive oil until translucent. Add peppers, onions, and garlic. Saute 2 minutes. Add shrimp and cook until firm. Add chicken stock and marinara. Season with fresh black pepper and chopped herbs. Before serving top with fresh grated Parmesan cheese. *Serves 4.*

This soup drops to only 13 percent fat calories if you eliminate the 1 tablespoon of olive oil.

Iron Horse Blanc de Blanc (California Sparkling)
Jacquart Brut Champagne (French Champagne)

GARNISH
   Fresh chopped herbs (basil, chives,
   parsley, thyme)
   Black pepper
   Parmesan cheese, grated

CRAB CAKES
with Strawberry Ginger Chutney and Curried Papaya Butter Sauce

BRAISED LAMB SHANKS
with Creamy Herb Polenta

KAHLUA CREME CARAMEL

Step through the door of 2808 Greenville Avenue, into an oasis and away from hectic Dallas life. The Grape is a comfortable reminder of Dallas wining and dining before the city's meteoric growth in the late '70s and '80s. Though revolutionary at the time, Dallas' first wine bistro, with its daily blackboard menu and emphasis on fine wine, has become a classic. We wish them a happy 20th anniversary this year.

Owners Kathy McDaniel and Charlotte Parker wax nostalgic as they look back to the inception of the restaurant, when the concept was just wine and cheese. "We signed a one-year lease with two one-year options. After the third year, we bought the building," says McDaniel. The Grape boasts a very large selection of Texas wines from 25 area wineries. Their total selection, which includes wines from Europe, Australia and South America, numbers well over 175 wines.

Parker says "We were the first restaurant in Dallas to sell wine by the glass, and we'll be the last to buy a microwave."

Through the years, their signature Fresh Mushroom Soup has been available daily on the chalkboard menu. The other items which appear offer diners a chance to dine lightly or enjoy a seven-course dinner. Meats, pasta and seafood dishes are determined daily by the availability of fresh foodstuffs.

Nowadays Parker is a nutritional counselor by day and creative mosaic-pottery artist by night. McDaniel is the managing partner in City Market, a downtown Dallas restaurant that caters for corporate and non-profit organizations. Parties of as many as 2,000 guests demand much of her time.

The Grape's unassuming facade gives no suggestion of the intimate atmosphere within its thick walls. Warm red and white checked tablecloths cover small, closely-set candlelit tables reminiscent of rural European restaurants. Comfortable chairs invite the eclectic dinner crowd to linger for conversation.

Customers flock from near and far, many for firsts visits, others to reminisce a first date or engagement at The Grape. This restaurant is consistently voted the most romantic in Dallas.

LITEFARE

Look for "Light of the Day" entree which features a moderate portion of chicken or fish with vegetables and starch. A vegetarian entree is also offered, usually pasta and vegetables. Dishes are seasoned with fresh herbs.

2808 Greenville Ave.
Dallas TX 75206
214/828-1981

CRAB CAKES
with Strawberry Ginger Chutney and Curried Papaya Butter Sauce

1 pound blue crabmeat, cleaned
1 small red onion, finely chopped
1/4 cup green onions, finely chopped
1 clove garlic, finely chopped
1 small red pepper, cut into small dice
1/2 cup mayonnaise
1 tablespoon Dijon mustard
1/4 cup small capers
1 cup white bread crumbs
1 tablespoon flour, plus flour for breading
   Dash Tabasco
   Dash Worcestershire sauce
   Dash salt and pepper
6 tablespoons butter

STRAWBERRY GINGER CHUTNEY
1 pound strawberries, halved and cleaned
2 tablespoons fresh ginger root, grated
2 tablespoons champagne vinegar
1/4 cup sugar
   Dash cayenne pepper

PAPAYA BUTTER SAUCE
1 papaya, peeled, seeded, cut into small dice
2 tablespoons minced shallots
1 teaspoon yellow curry
4 tablespoons butter
2 tablespoons sherry wine vinegar
1 cup white wine
1/4 cup heavy cream
1 pound unsalted butter
   Salt and white pepper to taste

Combine all ingredients except butter in a large mixing bowl. Form into 3-ounce, 1/2-inch thick cakes. Lightly flour and pan fry in butter until golden brown on both sides. Place crab cakes on a pool of papaya butter sauce and garnish with chutney and lemon wedges. *Serves 8.*

Strawberry Ginger Chutney
Place ingredients in medium-size saucepan and cook 30 to 35 minutes on medium high heat until nearly all liquid is reduced. Cool and serve.

Papaya Butter Sauce
Saute papaya, shallots and curry in the butter until tender. Deglaze pan with vinegar and white wine. Reduce liquid by half. Add cream and reduce over medium heat by half. Slowly add remaining butter while whipping constantly. Remove from heat and puree in blender 15 seconds. Strain through fine sieve and season with salt and white pepper.

 The chutney would make a low-fat and low-sodium accompaniment to any entree, but the Papaya Butter Sauce is very high in fat. Eliminate this sauce and you have a healthy, low-fat dish.

 Calera Viognier (California White)
Handley Cellars Gewurtztraminer (California White)

BRAISED LAMB SHANKS *with Creamy Herb Polenta*

6 pounds lamb shanks
1/2 cup olive oil
1/4 cup diced carrot
1/4 cup diced celery
1/4 cup chopped onion
1/4 cup sliced leek, white and
  pale green parts only
1 1/2 tablespoons minced garlic
1 cup red wine
4 cups veal stock
1 sprig fresh thyme
1 sprig fresh rosemary
1 bay leaf
1 tablespoon black peppercorns,
  cracked
4 tablespoons tomato paste
4 cups chicken stock
2 tablespoons unsalted butter
2 cups cornmeal
1 tablespoon chopped fresh herbs
  Salt and white pepper to taste

Preheat oven to 300 degrees. Sear lamb shanks in oil in saute pan. Transfer to roasting pan. Saute carrots, celery, onion, leeks and garlic for a few minutes in the same saute pan. Pour vegetables over lamb shanks, and add red wine, veal stock, herbs and cracked pepper. Cover roasting pan and braise for 2 hours in oven. Remove from oven and allow to cool in natural juices.

Prepare sauce by straining liquid into saucepan. Degrease. Whip in tomato paste and reduce to thicken. If desired, add sliced mushrooms and diced tomato.

Meanwhile, bring 4 cups chicken stock to boil, add unsalted butter and whip in cornmeal over medium heat. Cook 5 minutes and add chopped herbs, salt and white pepper. Present by spreading creamy polenta on platter. Place warmed lamb shank on top and nap lamb shank and plate with finished sauce. Garnish with fresh thyme and rosemary sprigs. *Serves 6.*

 Use lean lamb and eliminate extra fat by defatting the broth before reducing it for sauce.

 Chateau Haut-Bages Averous (French Red)
Swanson Cabernet Sauvignon (California Red)

KAHLUA CREME CARAMEL

2 cups sugar (divided use)
2 1/2 cups heavy cream
2 1/2 cups milk
1 vanilla bean or 1 teaspoon vanilla
   extract
6 eggs
6 egg yolks
4 tablespoons Kahlua liqueur

To line six individual charlotte molds with caramel: Dissolve 1/2 cup of sugar with 2 tablespoons water and divide into molds by swirling the water into the sugar (do not stir). Cover molds and place on low heat until sugar is completely dissolved. Uncover and raise heat. When desired caramel color is reached, remove from heat and plunge bottom of molds into cold water for a few seconds to stop the cooking. Swirl the caramel around the sides of the molds and invert onto a plate to cool.

Preheat oven to 325 degrees. Simmer the cream and milk with the vanilla for 5 minutes. Beat the remaining 1 1/2 cups sugar into the eggs and yolks and continue beating until the mixture is light and fluffy. Gradually add the Kahlua, hot milk, and cream, beating constantly. Strain the mixture into the prepared molds. Put the molds in a pan and pour boiling water into the pan to come halfway up the molds. Bake for about 45 minutes or until custard is firm. Cool.

To unmold, run a sharp knife around the edge of the custard. Put the serving dish over the mold and quickly invert. Pour the remaining caramel around the custard. *Serves 6.*

RED SNAPPER ALA JAVIER

RED SAUCE

GREEN SAUCE

BLACK BEAN SOUP

Bienvenido! to Mexico City cuisine. Javier Gutierrez brought genuine Mexican food to Dallas 15 years ago at his namesake restaurant, Javier's. Gutierrez was raised in Mexico City and moved to Dallas when he was 12. "The food here was totally different from what I was used to. People need to know more than Tex-Mex," says Gutierrez.

The unique chicken, seafood, beef and veal dishes have unusual chile peppers and seasoning combinations that impart new flavors to the Tex-Mex palate. The sauces have a long Mexican heritage, dating back to the Aztecs, with names like diablo, chile mulato and black pepper sauce.

Filete Cantinflas, a Cheese-stuffed Beef Tenderloin, and Red Snapper Mojo de Ajo, Red Snapper in Garlic and Lime Sauce, are house specialties. Many customers think the Ceviche is the best in Dallas, an exquisite combination of small shrimp, white fish, pico de gallo, lime and cilantro. The Shrimp Brochette Cozumel features a barbecue, pineapple and almond sauce which has a spicy, sweet and sour flavor combination unique to Dallas menus. Dessert selections include Cajeta (caramel made from goats milk) Crepes with sliced almonds and ice cream and Cafe Pierre which the waiters flambe tableside.

The comfortable, relaxed atmosphere of Javier's has its own flavor. Gutierrez has collected Spanish and Mexican artifacts and combined them with rough-hewn wood to give the feel of a Spanish Colonial public building.

Through the years, Javier's has become a Dallas institution, a place regular customers bring their out of town friends. He has shared his special red and green salsas in this book. Make both and enjoy them together the way they are served in the restaurant. Javier's, a 250-seat restaurant, is a testimonial unto itself; there is no restaurant row at Cole and Central Expressway. Guitierrez takes great pride in offering food so unusual that it is not found anywhere else in the country.

LiteFare

Mexico City cuisine offers lean meats, fish and chicken, accompanied by complex carbohydrates such as beans, rice and vegetables. The Bean Soup is low in fat, but refuse the added cheese and avocado. The black beans are refried, but the rice and vegetable accompaniments are steamed.

4912 Cole Avenue
Dallas TX 75205
214/521-4211

RED SNAPPER ALA JAVIER

3 tablespoons olive oil
1 medium onion, chopped
3 garlic cloves, minced
5 medium tomatoes, peeled and
    chopped (1 1/2 pounds)
10 Spanish-style green olives, pitted
    and chopped
2 tablespoons capers
3 bay leaves
6 peppercorns
    Salt
2 pounds red snapper fillets or other
    white fish fillets
    Salt

Heat olive oil in a large saucepan. Add onion and garlic. Cook until transparent but not browned. Add tomatoes, olives, capers, bay leaves, peppercorns and salt to taste. Bring to a boil; reduce heat. Simmer gently uncovered 10 minutes. Place fish fillets in a large skillet and sprinkle well with salt. Pour sauce over fish. Bring to a boil; reduce heat. Cover and simmer 10 minutes or until fish flakes easily when tested with a fork. *Serves 6.*

 Cut olive oil to 1 1/2 tablespoons and omit salt. There is plenty of salt in the olives and capers. This is a spicy, healthy preparation for a low-fat fish.

 Marques de Riscal Rioja Reserva (Spanish Red)
Renato Ratti Dolcetto d'Alba (Italian Red)

GREEN SAUCE

2 pounds tomatillos, husks removed
1 teaspoon chicken base or instant chicken bouillon
Pinch of oregano
2 bunches cilantro (leaves only) chopped
1 clove garlic, minced
1 teaspoon Worcestershire sauce
2 serrano peppers, seeded and chopped
1/4 cup chopped onions
1 tablespoon sugar or to taste

Soak tomatillos in warm water for 30 minutes. Cut up tomatillos and cover with water. Set aside for about 10 minutes or until tomatillos are tender. Drain.

Combine chicken base, oregano, cilantro, garlic, Worcestershire sauce, serrano peppers, onions and tomatillos. Put in a food processor or blender. Blend briefly until smooth. Return blender ingredients to saucepan, add sugar, and cook vigorously over medium heat for 30 minutes. If tomatillos are very acid, add more sugar. *Makes 2 quarts.*

 Zesty, low-fat and low-sodium sauce.

 Houtz Sauvignon Blanc (California White)
Mondavi Fume Blanc (California White)

RED SAUCE

2 pounds tomatoes
1/8 cup vegetable oil
1 teaspoon salt
1 clove garlic, minced
1 tablespoon cayenne pepper (add more for hotter sauce)
1 teaspoon chicken base or instant chicken boullion

Peel and core tomatoes. Place tomatoes in a large pot with just enough boiling water to cover. Cook until tender; drain. Place tomatoes in a blender or food processor. Blend until texture is smooth. Add oil to medium size saucepan. Place over medium heat. When oil is hot, add blended tomatoes, salt, garlic, ground red pepper to taste, and chicken base. Bring to a boil, reduce heat slightly and cook vigorously for 30 minutes. Remove from heat and skim foam from top. *Makes 2 quarts.*

 Eliminate the oil and you have a healthy low-fat sauce.

 Pedroncelli Zinfandel (California Red)

BLACK BEAN SOUP

1/2 **pound black beans**
1/2 **onion**
  1 **clove garlic**
  4 **teaspoons olive oil, divided use**
  2 **teaspoons onion, chopped**
  2 **tomatoes, pureed**
    Salt to taste
1/2 **cup Monterey Jack cheese, grated,**
    for garnish
    Avocado slices for garnish

Wash beans and soak in cold water overnight. In a pressure cooker, cook the beans, with 1/2 onion, garlic, salt and 1 teaspoon of olive oil for 1 hour. When beans are cooked and cooled, put in a blender and puree.

In a casserole dish, warm 3 teaspoons of olive oil. Cook chopped onion until transparent, add blended tomatoes and cook, adding salt until well-seasoned. Add the bean puree. If mixture is too thick add some water. Cook for about 10 minutes on low temperature. Serve hot. Add grated cheese on top. Avocado slice optional. *Serves 6.*

 This is a low-fat soup without the added cheese and avocado.

 McDowell Valley Syrah (California Red)
Clos du Val Zinfandel (California Red)

JUNIPER ROAST CHICKEN
MEDALLIONS DE VEAU AU CITRON VERT
JUNIPER ROQUEFORT CHEESE POTATOES
VEGETABLE TART NIÇOISE

Partners Nancilee Foree and Chef Christian Gerber have restored a charming 90-year old cottage in an area of Dallas which was known as "the vineyard." It is the perfect setting for the robust flavors of Provence. The comforting aroma of a constantly bubbling stockpot subtly prepares the diner for his country French meal. The intimate dining rooms inside are bright white and forest green, with large windows overlooking the tree-shaded patio where al fresco dining is available seasonally.

"The trend in food today is to go back to regional basics in France as well as in America," says Gerber. Signature dishes such as Sauteed Wild Mushrooms in Tarragon and Muscat Wine Sauce, Roasted Country Chicken With Garlic and Herbs de Provence, Fresh Grilled Vegetables With Aioli, and Hot Apple Tart, show the nature of the menu.

At Juniper, olive oils, lavender, fresh herbs, and pungent garlic are as much a part of the kitchen as they are the countryside of Provence. The cuisine reflects Foree's attitude concerning food. "Food really shouldn't be too serious. I like real food, prepared with integrity," she says.

"My cooking is simple," says Gerber. "I research regional French cookbooks of the past and revive and enhance classic recipes. I will use only the best quality of fresh ingredients, which allows the true flavor of the dish to emerge, enhanced with natural reduction sauces." These sauces contain no starch or flour, only natural flavors.

Christian Gerber trained in France before coming to The Old Warsaw as a sous chef in 1973. He worked at La Caravelle in New York, but returned to Dallas a year later to work, once again, at The Old Warsaw as Chef de Cuisine. He has remained in Dallas since then staying busy as a teacher, consultant, private caterer and restaurateur. He maintains an extensive antique cookbook collection which began 30 years ago. It has been loaned to various institutions, including the Dallas Public Library. Chef Gerber also plays soccer as passionately as he cooks.

LITEFARE

Try the Pistou de Provence, Fresh Grilled Vegetables or any of the grilled fish. Most soups are stock-based and are not thickened with cream.

2917 Fairmont Street
Dallas TX 75201
214/855-0700

JUNIPER ROAST CHICKEN

1   2 1/2-pound chicken
4-6 cloves garlic
1   tablespoon herbes de Provence
    Fresh thyme
    Fresh oregano
    Fresh rosemary
    Fresh sage
    Fresh tarragon
    Freshly ground pepper
    Salt
1   tablespoon olive oil
1   tablespoon butter
1   cup white wine
1   tablespoon tomato paste
2   cups chicken stock

Preheat oven to 400 degrees. Chop the garlic and herbs, rub inside and outside of chicken with herb mixture, reserving one teaspoon. Season chicken with salt and pepper. Heat the oil and butter together in a roasting pan until sizzling. Sear the chicken on all sides. Put the chicken into the preheated oven and roast about 45 minutes. Debone. Remove fat from the roasting pan, put bones back into the roasting pan. Add the tomato paste and deglaze with the white wine. Reduce for a few minutes; add the chicken stock and reduce again. Strain into a small saucepan. Saute remaining herb and garlic mixture in olive oil until garlic is slightly browned, and add to sauce pan. Reduce until sauce thickens. Pour generously over the roasted chicken. *Serves 2 to 4.*

 Cook chicken in its skin to retain moisture, but remove skin before eating for a low-fat dish.

 Firestone Pinot Noir (California Red)
Sanford Pinot Noir (California Red)

MEDALLIONS DE VEAU AU CITRON VERT

4 thick 2-ounce slices cut from the
  filet of trimmed veal
1 tablespoon oil
1 tablespoon butter
2 tablespoons white wine
  Juice of 2 limes
1 cup of veal stock*
1 shallot, minced
1/2 teaspoon meat glaze
  (glace de viande)**
1 teaspoon butter
  Sliced lime and watercress for
  garnish

Season veal and saute in hot oil and butter for a few minutes. Remove to a warm platter. Add shallots and saute for a few seconds, then deglaze the pan with white wine and lime juice. Add veal stock and reduce until sauce has the proper consistency. Correct seasoning and strain sauce. Finish with meat glaze and butter. If necessary add more lime juice. Pour sauce around veal and garnish with sliced lime and watercress. *Serves 2.*

* Chef Gerber recommends homemade veal stock. Juniper is happy for anyone to purchase veal stock from the restaurant.
** Meat glaze is veal stock reduced to a thick concentrate.

 Veal is a lean meat. Limit oil and butter for sauteeing veal to 1 teaspoon each. Pour any excess oil off before deglazing pan. Omit adding last teaspoon of butter to sauce.

 Estancia Chardonnay (California White)
Williams Selyem Pinot Noir (California Red)

JUNIPER ROQUEFORT CHEESE POTATOES

1 tablespoon oil
2 tablespoons butter, plus butter for
  sheet pan
2 tablespoons garlic puree
2 tablespoons finely chopped shallots
6 ounces Roquefort cheese
1 1/2 pounds new potatoes, thinly sliced
  and patted dry withpaper towels
  White pepper
2 cups heavy cream
1/3 cup milk
3 ounces Parmesan cheese

Preheat oven to 350 degrees. In a large roasting pan heat oil and butter and add garlic and shallots. Sweat by cooking on top of the stove. Add Roquefort cheese and melt over low flame. Add the potatoes and a pinch of white pepper. Pour the cream and milk into the pan and bring to a boil, stirring, for two minutes. Add the Parmesan cheese and take off the heat source. Butter a 17-by-13-inch sheet pan and spread potato mixture onto sheet pan. Bake for 30 minutes or until golden brown. *Serves 2 to 4.*

 R. H. Phillips Night Harvest Cuvee Rouge (California Red)
Stonestreet Chardonnay (California White)

VEGETABLE TART NIÇOISE

1 10-by-15-inch sheet of puff pastry
1/2 cup tomato-basil coulis
     (recipe follows)
4 cloves garlic, minced (divided use)
3 ripe tomatoes, thinly sliced
2 medium zucchini, thinly sliced
2 medium eggplant, thinly sliced
2 medium yellow squash, thinly sliced
2 medium carrots, thinly sliced
4 tablespoons olive oil
1 tablespoon herbes de Provence*
Salt and pepper
1 cup fresh basil leaves cut into
   julienne
1/2 cup black nicoise olives
1/2 cup Parmesan cheese

TOMATO-BASIL COULIS

3 ripe tomatoes
1 shallot
1/2 clove garlic
1 tablespoon olive oil
1 cup fresh basil leaves cut into
   julienne
1 cup chicken stock
1 tablespoon butter

Preheat oven to 375 degrees. Line a sheet pan with parchment paper. Place the pastry in the pan and spread lightly with tomato-basil coulis and 1/2 of the chopped garlic. Arrange the tomatoes, zucchini, eggplant, yellow squash and carrots overlapping in alternate rows. Drizzle with olive oil and remaining chopped garlic, herbes de Provence and season to taste with salt and pepper. Bake until vegetables are just tender and pastry is crisp. Serve on a bed of tomato-basil coulis. Garnish with julienne of basil, olives and Parmesan cheese. *Serves 8-10.*

* Herbes de Provence is a mixture of various herbs such as basil, thyme, fennel seed, sage, rosemary and marjoram.

Tomato-basil Coulis
Saute tomatoes, shallot, garlic and basil in the olive oil for a few minutes. Add chicken stock and cook for 10 minutes. Puree in food processor. Strain the sauce, and reduce for a few minutes if not thick enough. Correct seasonings and finish with 1 tablespoon butter.

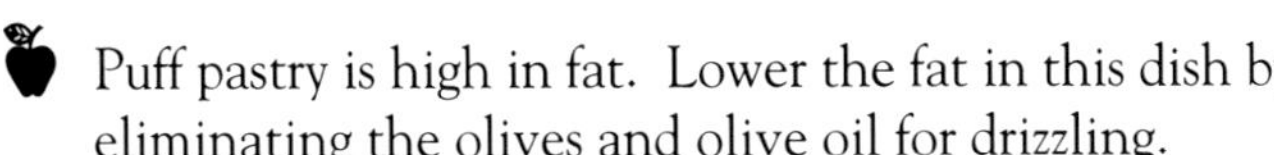 Puff pastry is high in fat. Lower the fat in this dish by eliminating the olives and olive oil for drizzling.

 Buena Vista Sauvignon Blanc (California White)
Frescobaldi Tenuta di Pomino (Italian Red)

FACING PAGE, *from left:*
Vivian Young, Caroline Rose Hunt, Lady Primrose's;
Javier Gutierrez, Javier's; Christian Gerber, Juniper

FOLLOWING PAGE, *from left: Ron Rosenbaum, Nana Grill;*
Helmut Wesemann, Mi Piaci

LOEWS ANATOLE HOTEL
Ronald Rosenb
NANA GRILL
Mi Piaci
Executive Chef
Helmut Wesemann

MOTHER HUBBARD'S SQUASH SOUP

SHEPHERD'S PIE

SCOTCH EGGS

THORNBURY CASTLE SPONGE
with Walnut Toffee Sauce

CHICKEN BOMBAY SANDWICH

PEAR & STILTON SANDWICH

The English ceremonial art of "Tea" is practiced in award-winning high style at Lady Primrose's Thatched Cottage Pantry. Four years ago co-owners Caroline Rose Hunt and Vivian Young added authentic English recipes for tea and lunch to their antique store. "The whole idea is to step back, sit down and have a civilized cup of tea," says Young. "It will refresh your mental and physical state."

Afternoon tea is traditionally served from three until five at Lady Primrose's. A welcoming mood is cast by the four imaginative thatched cottages upstairs. The vision is enhanced by richly draped tables set with fresh flowers, vases of celery and carrot sticks, and fine English china.

The aromas of Primrose's custom-blended teas and the charming presentation of light foods offer a variety of shape, color, taste, and texture. Customer's spirits are lifted as well. Stacked scones with homemade clotted cream and jam, cakes and decorated cookies, and an assortment of sandwiches are offered with choices of tea. Secret Garden, a blend of peaches, cinnamon and hibiscus flowers, Lady Caroline, finished with strawberry and mint, and Herbal Garden, a blend of fruit and herbs, are among the selection.

Tea is carefully poured through a strainer into a warm cup and hot water is added for the desired strength. Milk or lemon and sugar is passed. Tea served in this graceful fashion builds friendship among strangers and makes good friends even better friends.

The 45-seat tearoom's popularity has blossomed, and Lady Primrose's must sometimes turn away thirsty tea-takers. Lady Primrose's was recently recognized as the best tearoom in a United States hotel by the highly regarded Tea Quarterly magazine.

SHOPPING ENGLISH COUNTRYSIDE

Lady Primrose's

LITEFARE

The wonderful assortment of teas at this English tearoom are all low-fat and stimulating. The accompaniments need to be chosen with care. Best bet is the scone with jam, but skip the clotted cream.

500 Crescent Court
Dallas, TX 75201
214/871-8334

MOTHER HUBBARD'S SQUASH SOUP

1 medium onion, chopped
2 cloves garlic, minced
1 tablespoon margarine
1/2 teaspoon freshly ground white pepper
Salt to taste
2 1/2 cups chicken stock
3 pounds winter squash (hubbard, butternut or acorn) peeled, seeded and diced
2 cups milk
Dash nutmeg

Saute the onions and garlic in margarine until transparent. Add pepper, broth, squash and salt; bring liquid to a boil for 15 minutes. Remove from heat and stir in milk and nutmeg. Puree soup in blender, return to heat, but do not boil. *Serves 10.*

 This delicious soup is only 25 percent fat calories when made with whole milk. Use low-fat or skim milk to further reduce fat.

 Piper Sonoma Brut (California Sparkling)
Ferrari-Carano Chardonnay (California White)

SHEPHERD'S PIE

1 medium yellow onion, chopped
3 cloves garlic, minced
3 tablespoons canola oil
1 pound lean beef, cut from the round, cut into 1 1/2-inch cubes
3 tablespoons flour
1 pint beef stock
2 pounds potatoes, peeled and diced (divided use)
1 cup diced carrots
1 cup green peas
1 cup sliced mushrooms
6 tablespoons butter
1 cup milk
1 ounce grated cheddar cheese
Dash Worcestershire sauce
Salt and pepper

Heat the oil in a medium-size heavy bottomed sauce pot until smoking. Add beef and sear well on all sides. Reduce heat and add onion. Saute 20 seconds, then add garlic. Stir in flour, cook until it begins to brown. Add beef stock and bring to a boil. After 10 minutes reduce to simmer and add 1/2 pound of potatoes and all the carrots, cooking for 30 minutes. While the meat and vegetables are simmering, boil the reserved potato, drain and mash with the butter and milk. Put the meat mixture in a large casserole dish or in individual dishes, cover with mashed potatoes. Sprinkle with cheese and bake at 400 degrees for 15 to 20 minutes of until golden. *Serves 6.*

 Sear beef in pan sprayed with no-stick cooking spray. Substitute low-fat milk and 3 tablespoons margarine for butter.

 Pheasant Ridge Cabernet Sauvignon Blackmon Vineyard (Texas Red)
Torres Coronas (Spanish Red)

SCOTCH EGGS

8 hard-boiled eggs
1/4 cup flour
1 1/2 pounds ground sausage
2 cups seasoned bread crumbs
2 eggs, beaten

Peel hard-boiled eggs then roll in flour. Take sausage and shape into eight equal flat patties, then completely cover the egg. Seal firmly and form into egg shape. Repeat with remaining 7 eggs.

Roll the sausage-coated eggs in flour. Brush with beaten eggs and roll to coat in seasoned bread crumbs. Deep-fry Scotch eggs for 10 minutes, or shallow-fry for 15 minutes, turning often; or bake on a lightly greased cookie sheet in a 400-degree preheated oven. Serve hot or cold. *Serves 8.*

 Use low-fat turkey sausage; substitute 4 egg whites for whole eggs to coat eggs; bake in oven rather than frying.

 Deutz Champagne (French Champagne)
Gloria Ferrer Brut (California Sparkling)

THORNBURY CASTLE SPONGE *with Walnut Toffee Sauce*

1 stick butter (divided use)
3/4 cup granulated sugar
1 teaspoon vanilla extract
2 teaspoons baking powder
2 cups self-rising flour
2 eggs, well beaten
3/4 cup boiling water
1 1/3 cups dried dates, chopped
Flour, to dust
1/2 cup firmly packed brown sugar
2/3 cup heavy cream
1/2 cup shelled walnuts
Whiskey or rum, optional
Unsweetened whipped cream

To prepare the sponge, beat 1/2 stick butter, granulated sugar, and vanilla to a cream. Mix the baking powder with the flour and add with the eggs gradually to the butter and sugar. Add boiling water. Toss the dried dates in a little flour and add to the batter. Pour into a well-buttered or non-stick 10-inch baking tin and cook in a hot oven (360 degrees) for about 40 minutes or until a skewer comes out clean.

To prepare the sauce, melt the remaining 1/2 stick butter, add brown sugar, cream and walnuts. Add a little whiskey or rum if desired. Bring to a boil.

Serve slices of the hot sponge covered with very hot sauce and cold thick cream. *Makes one 10-inch cake.*

CHICKEN BOMBAY SANDWICHES

2 cups cooked chicken breast, slivered
1/2 cup cooked and minced bacon
3/4 cup grated white cheddar cheese
1/4 cup red bell pepper, seeded, cleaned and diced
2 tablespoons minced green onion
Salt and pepper
1 1/2 tablespoons Madras curry powder
1/2 teaspoon ground turmeric
1 teaspoon minced garlic
Dash Tabasco sauce
1/2 cup mayonnaise

In a bowl combine slivered chicken breast, bacon, cheese, red bell pepper and green onion, and toss together. Add salt, pepper, curry powder, turmeric, garlic and Tabasco. Then add enough mayonnaise to bind to desired consistency. *Makes 12 sandwiches.*

 To lower the fat, eliminate the bacon, substitute light mayonnaise for regular, and use low-fat cheddar cheese.

 Bartlett Blueberry Wine (Maine Red)
Hugel Riesling (French White)

PEAR AND STILTON SANDWICHES

8 slices grainy bread, toasted
5 pears, thinly sliced
3 cups Sandeman Port
8 ounces Stilton cheese, crumbled slightly
Watercress for garnish

Core pears and cut into 1/4-inch slices horizontally. Put in shallow dish and cover with Port; let stand for one hour. Drain pears and arrange on toasted bread. Top with one ounce (2 tablespoons) of Stilton on each sandwich and place in oven for 10 minutes at 350 degrees. Serve on a bed of watercress. *Serves 8.*

 Sandwich is fairly low in fat. To cut fat, reduce cheese to 4 ounces, 1/2 ounce per sandwich.

 Rayne Vigneau Sauternes (French dessert wine)
Sandeman Port (Portugese fortified wine)

MI PIACI

OSSO BUCO MILANESE

SAFFRON RISOTTO

LEMON GELATO

SALMONE AL SALMORIGLIO

INSALATA DI CARCIOFI

Sunbeams glint across the shimmering waters of Preston Pond, flooding Mi Piaci with golden light. This beautiful Addison restaurant won the *Architectural Digest's* 1991 award for restaurant design.

As in Italy, the diner is greeted with a display of appetizing dishes and the ambience of a contemporary trattoria. Huge windows overlook the landmark pond on the recaptured farmland. Inside, swirled columns lift the eye to a domed ceiling.

In this glowing environ, Executive Chef Helmut Wesemann produces delicately flavored, authentic Italian food. Bruschetta al Pomodoro (grilled bread topped with tomato) prepares the palate for delicate homemade pastas such as Strangozzi alla Pirate, a generous portion of fresh spaghetti with shellfish and delicately spiced tomato sauce. The Caprese Classica, Osso Buco and Lobster Risotto are three of the most popular dishes Wesemann prepares in Mi Piaci's enormous, well-equipped kitchens.

Health-conscious diners may choose from several dishes prepared with low-fat, cholesterol-free imported dry pastas and seafood, vegetable or herb sauces.

"I love to work with the best ingredients," says Wesemann. "The Italian way of cooking is very balanced. You don't use excessive oil, and sauces are straightforward with chicken broth and vegetables." Chef Wesemann prepares special meals not on the menu, filling requests for "linguini with some mushrooms" for example, to satisfy a recent diner's craving.

Like many fine chefs, Wesemann was a music major in college. He received his chef's training in Switzerland, and worked for seven years in California before coming to Dallas.

Mi Piaci offers private dining in rooms as beautiful as its main dining area. The wine cellar dining room downstairs is accessed by a spiral staircase. Upstairs a small dining room has French doors which open onto a lovely patio. Upon request, lunch or dinner may be served al fresco.

For all its style, Mi Piaci is an unpretentious restaurant. Patrons wear anything from evening clothes to jeans, even on Saturday nights.

--- LITEFARE ---

Two complex carbohydrates, pasta and risotto, are specialties of Mi Piaci. Combine them with a low-fat sauce, such Pomodoro or Spicy Tomato. Skip the Tuscan bread and have crispy breadsticks.

14854 Montfort
Dallas, TX 75240
214/934-8424

OSSO BUCO MILANESE

1/3　cup vegetable oil
　4　pounds veal shanks
1/2　cup unbleached flour
2/3　cup unsalted butter
　1　cup chopped yellow onions
　1　large carrot, chopped
2/3　cup chopped celery
　4　cloves garlic, peeled
1/2　teaspoon lemon zest
3/4　cup dry white wine
　1　cup plus 2 tablespoons veal broth*
3/4　cup canned plum tomatoes
　3　sprigs fresh thyme
　3　sprigs Italian parsley
　2　tablespoons chopped fresh basil
　　　Pinch sea salt
　　　Pinch black pepper
　4　cups saffron risotto (recipe follows)
　1　tablespoon Parmesan rocca cheese

Choose a heavy casserole with a tight-fitting lid that will accommodate the veal shanks later. Heat the vegetable oil over medium-high heat. Dip the shanks on both sides in flour, shake off excess and brown each side well. Remove the shanks from the casserole, add the butter, onions, carrots, celery and saute over low heat until they are soft and light brown. Add the garlic, lemon zest and stir a couple of times.

Deglaze the pan with white wine and loosen all residue from the bottom of the pan. Let the wine reduce over high heat for 3 to 5 minutes. Place the shanks back into the casserole. Pour just enough veal broth to barely cover the shanks, add the chopped tomatoes, thyme, parsley, basil, and season with salt and crushed black pepper. Let the broth come to a simmer. Put the lid on and place the casserole in the preheated oven at 350 degrees for 1 1/2 to 2 hours. About every 30 minutes, turn the shanks. When meat is tender and almost falls off the bone the Osso Buco is ready. If the sauce is not of a creamy consistency you can reduce it over high heat after removing the shanks. *Serves 4.*

* Veal stock is available frozen in many local supermarkets.

 Eliminate the butter and saute vegetables in the vegetable oil left in the pan. This recipe with the Saffron Risotto is then only 37 percent fat calories.

 Tenuta Marchese Antinori Riserva Chianti Classico (Italian Red)
Granduca Barolo (Italian Red)

SAFFRON RISOTTO

8 cups chicken broth
3/4 teaspoon saffron
5 tablespoons unsalted butter
(divided use)
1 pound arborio rice
3/4 teaspoon sea salt
3/4 teaspoon black pepper
1 cup shredded Parmesan cheese

Bring chicken broth to a simmer and add saffron. Let simmer for a few minutes until broth turns dark golden. Put 2 tablespoons butter into a pot, add the rice and stir over medium heat until the rice is evenly covered with butter. Deglaze the rice with one cup of broth, stirring. When broth is all absorbed by the rice, add another cup.

Turn the heat down to a slow simmer, keep stirring the rice and adding broth when almost all of it is absorbed.

When rice is done and has reached a creamy consistency, stop adding broth. Add salt and black pepper, the remaining butter, and Parmesan cheese. Remove risotto from the heat and serve immediately. *Serves 4.*

 Risotto is a complex carbohydrate and this recipe is low in total fat. Use low-fat and low-sodium chicken stock, and omit added salt.

 Hess Collection Chardonnay (California White)
Centine Rosso di Montalcino (Italian Red)

LEMON GELATO

1 3/4 cups cold water
1 1/8 cups granulated sugar
1 1/2 teaspoons lemon zest
3/4 cup fresh lemon juice
1/3 cup heavy cream

Heat water to the boiling point, add sugar and stir until dissolved. Add lemon zest and lemon juice and let mixture cool. Strain through a very fine sieve. Add mixture to the ice-cream machine and freeze, following manufacturers instructions. Five to ten minutes before the Lemon Gelato is finished, add the heavy cream. *Makes one quart.*

 This is a low-fat dessert even with the addition of the cream.

SALMONE AL SALMORIGLIO

4 teaspoons fresh oregano leaves,
    picked from stems
1/2 cup extra-virgin olive oil
4 teaspoons fresh-squeezed
    lemon juice
1 teaspoon black pepper
4 7-ounce Norwegian salmon steaks
2 teaspoons sea salt
    Seasonal vegetables
4 roasted potatoes*

Add the oregano leaves to the olive oil with lemon juice and a touch of cracked pepper. Rub the salmon steaks lightly with olive oil mixture. Grill over medium heat. Season when finished with salt and pour one tablespoon of the sauce over each salmon steak. Serve with roasted potatoes and vegetables. *Serves 4.*

* Roast the potatoes in the oven with chopped garlic, fresh rosemary, extra-virgin olive oil, salt and pepper.

 Salmon is a medium fat fish, and the added olive oil makes this dish high in fat. Use as little oil as possible. Nutrition information is without vegetables and potato.

 Knudsen Erath Pinot Noir (Oregon Red)
Le Chamville Beaujolais (French Red)

INSALATA DI CARCIOFI

1 pound arugula
1 pound fresh baby artichokes
4 tablespoons extra-virgin olive oil
1 1/2 cups shredded Parmesan cheese
    Pinch sea salt
    Pinch black pepper
2 lemons, juiced (divided use)

Wash arugula and drain in a colander. Remove the outer green leaves of the baby artichokes until only the yellow leaves remain. Cut the stem off and slice the artichoke very thin. To prevent the slices from turning black, keep them in lemon water made with the juice of one lemon.

In a bowl, toss the arugula, the slices of baby artichokes (squeeze them dry when you take them out of the lemon water), the remaining lemon juice, the olive oil, salt and pepper. Place tossed salad on a plate and sprinkle with shaved Parmesan cheese. *Serves 4.*

 Cut the Parmesan cheese to 1/2 cup and the olive oil to 1 tablespoon to bring the fat calories down to 33 percent.

 Santa Sofia Soave Classico Superiore (Italian White)
Regaleali Bianco (Italian White)

SHE CRAB SOUP

SWORDFISH AND MARINATED PEPPERS
with Eggplant Chips

LOBSTER & YELLOW TOMATO BISQUE
with Lobster Pico de Gallo

Dazzling city lights twinkle beyond the broad windows of the elegant Nana Grill, high atop the Loews Anatole Hotel where Chef Ron Rosenbaum dishes up hearty, sophisticated fare.

Chef Rosenbaum says, "Flavor is my key word. Whatever ethnic sauce I come up with for the grilled fish special always sells well. His menus offer incredible renditions of fresh fish, like Red Snapper With Sauteed Lump Crabmeat and Missouri Ham, and beef such as the One Pound Kansas City Sirloin With Maytag Bleu Cheese Butter. A knock-out array of appetizers and salads tempts diners with Honey Glazed Grilled Shrimp and delectable Field Greens with Goat Cheese Fritter.

Rosenbaum worked and learned in the kitchens of The Mansion on Turtle Creek and the Adolphus Hotel before joining The Anatole three and a half years ago. He has unleashed his creativity in Nana Grill. "Eighty to ninety percent of cooking is in learned skills and practice, while ten to twenty percent is artistic freedom," Rosenbaum says.

He exercises this artistic freedom quite well, creating dishes which please both eye and palate. He works constantly to develop new dishes and delight diners.

"I've always been a rebel. I personally try to go against the trends. Everyone's new favorite ingredient is sun-dried tomatoes. Even though I love them, I try not to use them."

Rosenbaum's creative philosophy is tempered with knowledge of his customers' desires. He believes it is important to offer meat and potatoes meals to satisfy less adventurous palates.

Nana Grill boasts a companion bar with an equally stunning view of the city and of "Nana," the famous life-size portrait the bar is named after. Artist Gospodin Suchorowsky completed the six by nine-foot canvas in 1881.

LITEFARE

Serving sizes of meat, fish and fowl are generous, but chef will split portions. Special requests are encouraged. A grilled or steamed vegetable plate can be prepared upon request.

The Loews Anatole Hotel
2201 Stemmons Frwy.
Dallas, TX 75207
214/748-1200

SHE CRAB SOUP

3 cups heavy whipping cream
2 tablespoons butter
4 ounces fresh shallots, peeled and
    sliced
1 whole leek, white part only, washed
    and dried, rough chopped
1 bunch fresh thyme (divided use)
16 ounces Tio Pepe Sherry*
46 ounces canned clam juice
    Old Bay Seafood Seasoning**
2 tablespoons cornstarch
1 pound fresh crabmeat, cleaned of
    cartilage and shell
2 hard-boiled egg yolks, pushed
    through a fine sieve
1 bunch fresh chives, minced

In a heavy saucepan, reduce heavy whipping cream by half until sauce consistency is achieved. Set aside.
Heat another saucepan over medium heat until moderately hot. Add butter and when it reaches the bubbling point, saute shallots, leek and half of thyme until soft. Add sherry, bring heat to high and cook sherry at a full boil until almost dry.

Pour clam juice into sherry and shallot mixture and bring to simmer. Add reduced heavy whipping cream and again bring to a simmer.

At this point, add remaining thyme, Old Bay to taste and salt if necessary. Make a cornstarch slurry by mixing approximately 2 tablespoons of water and 2 tablespoons of cornstarch. Add this slowly, letting soup come to a boil, until a nice creamy thickness is achieved. Strain through a fine sieve and hold hot until served. *Yields approximately 3 quarts and serves 12.*

Ladle soup into bowls and garnish with crabmeat, crumbled egg yolk and finely cut chives.

 * This brand works best, but you can substitute Dry Sack or other brands if necessary.

** This item should be available in specialty grocery stores in your area. If not, use your own favorite brand. Old Bay is a traditional East Coast product.

 Lungarotti Pinot Grigio (Italian White)
Chalk Hill Chardonnay (California White)

SWORDFISH AND MARINATED PEPPERS *with Eggplant Chips*

2 red bell peppers, roasted, seeded, cut into julienne
2 yellow bell peppers, roasted, seeded, cut into julienne
2 poblano peppers, roasted, seeded, cut into julienne
2 shallots, minced
2 anchovy fillets, very finely chopped
3 fresh jalapenos, seeded, very finely chopped
1/2 cup rich lobster stock*
1/2 cup extra-virgin olive oil
1/4 cup sushi or rice vinegar
2 tablespoons fresh lime juice
1 teaspoon freshly cracked black pepper
1/2 teaspoon Kosher salt
2 tablespoons pure maple syrup
15 leaves fresh basil, chopped
15 sprigs Italian parsley, minced
1/2 bunch chives, minced
15 sprigs cilantro, chopped

1 pound Japanese eggplant, sliced as thin as possible
Rice flour seasoned with salt and pepper
Vegetable oil at 250 degrees for frying eggplant chips

4 7 1/2-ounce center cut swordfish steaks, keep chilled until ready to cook

To roast peppers, put in 450-degree oven on foil until skins are partially black. Remove from oven, place in paper bag to sweat for five minutes. Remove charred peel and set aside. Combine remaining ingredients in a mixing bowl and add peppers. Chill for 2 hours and adjust seasoning if necessary. Hold chilled for service.

As the eggplant chips are sliced, toss in seasoned rice flour. This helps avoid discoloration. Fry at 250 degrees until the chips float to top of oil (just before they start browning). Remove with slotted spoon and drain on paper towels. The chips will be slightly crisp at this time and will continue to crisp up as they dry out. Keep in a warm place until service.

To serve, oil and season swordfish steaks and grill to desired doneness. Divide marinated pepper mixture on 4 large plates. Place swordfish on top and sprinkle eggplant chips around the fish. Garnish with sprigs of fresh herbs as desired. *Serves 4.*

* Rich lobster stock is raw shrimp, lobster heads, bodies and shells seared over high heat in olive oil with mirepoix and covered with chicken stock.

 Swordfish is moderate in fat. Eliminate the Eggplant Chips, omit oiling the fish before grilling, and use only 1 tablespoon of oil for the marinated peppers to reduce the fat calories to 31 percent. Salt can also be eliminated.

 Iron Horse Fume Blanc (California White)
Foxen Pinot Noir (California Red)

LOBSTER AND YELLOW TOMATO BISQUE *with Lobster Pico de Gallo*

1 yellow bell pepper, seeded, rough cut
2 yellow onions, peeled, rough cut
2 leeks, white part only, rough cut
10 cloves garlic, peeled
4 pounds yellow tomatoes, rough cut
1 medium sweet potato, peeled, rough cut
1/2 teaspoon saffron

Bouquet Garni
2 bunches fresh basil
1 bunch fresh thyme
1 bunch fresh tarragon
1 jalapeno pepper
10 white peppercorns
1 bay leaf

1 inch piece of fresh ginger, peeled and rough cut
2 cups dry white wine
1 cup white port
1 cup brandy
1 quart white lobster stock
1 1/2 pounds unsalted butter (divided use)
2 cups heavy whipping cream, reduced by half
Kosher salt to taste
1/4 teaspoon cayenne pepper
1/2 teaspoon Old Bay Seafood Seasoning
Juice of 3 limes

In a large stainless steel saucepan, saute the yellow bell pepper, yellow onions, leeks and garlic in 1/2 pound butter until soft. Add yellow tomatoes, sweet potato, saffron, bouquet garni, ginger, dry white wine, white port and brandy and cook until almost dry. Add white lobster stock and bring to a boil. Simmer 30 minutes while reducing heavy cream by half in a separate non-reactive pan. Remove bouquet garni and blend soup, reduced cream and remaining butter in blender. Skim foam after passing through a fine sieve. Season to taste with kosher salt, cayenne and Old Bay. Finish with freshly squeezed lime juice. *Serves 12.*

Lobster Pico De Gallo
12 ounces cooked lobster meat, cut into 1/4-inch dice
1 fresh jalapeno, seeded, very finely diced
15 sprigs cilantro, chopped
6 ounces tomatoes, peeled, seeded and diced
6 ounces jicama, peeled, finely diced
Kosher salt to taste
1 bunch chives, very finely cut

Combine above ingredients and season to taste with kosher salt. To serve, ladle hot soup into heated soup bowls and spoon 1 tablespoon of Lobster Pico de Gallo on top of each bowlful.

 Lobster Pico de Gallo is very low in fat. It could be used as a spread with melba toast.

 Beringer Chardonnay (California White)
Merryvale Meritage (California White)

POLENTA PASTICCIATA CON SALSICCE

PAPPA AL POMODORO

POMODORO CHEESECAKE

RISOTTO CON LASELLA DEL CONIGLIO

Lori and Efisio Farris invite you to Pomodoro and Arcodoro Bar, the Cedar Springs restaurants that love built.

The Farrises met in Manhattan, while seated next to one another at a west side Italian restaurant. Both were vacationing in New York City. She was from Chicago, and he was visiting from his native Sardinia. They have been business partners since the beginning, but their wedding had to wait five years.

In that time, Pomodoro was founded and a sibling restaurant Arcodoro Bar recently opened. Both will soothe your craving for the feel and flavor of Italian food, drink and art. Authentic Tuscan and Sardinian food is homemade from recipes handed down through generations of their families.

Dallas diners should gauge the time of day and their appetites to select one of these restaurants. Hungry patrons will fare well with one of 22 pasta selections from Pomodoro's comprehensive menu, while lighter appetites will be satisfied with pastries, pizza, panini and focaccia that Arcodoro offers.

For the famished diner, two such dishes at Pomodoro are Lasagne al Sugo di Caccia (lasagna with game sauce), and Panzotti del Passante (half moon pasta stuffed with seafood in a pistachio cream sauce). Pomodoro displays Mr. Farris's tempting collection of grappa, a clear spirit distilled from grape stems and skins.

"Arcodoro is what a European bar is - a place to come for coffee or cappuccino, to meet friends or business associates and pass time," says Mr. Farris. Arcodoro starts the day with breakfast and keeps the custom-made wood-burning tile oven busy morning and night baking delicious specialties.

The restaurants share the same Italian wine list and the same chef. Until Chef Salvatore Gisellu arrived from Italy a year ago, Mr. Farris cooked. When asked how he manages two kitchens., Gisellu replies, "No limits for Italians."

LiteFare

Pomodoro: Healthful carbohydrates (pasta and risotto) are featured on this menu. Order the Integrali Primavera, wheat noodles with fresh vegetables in tomato sauce.

Arcodoro Bar: Pizza can be healthy and low fat with the right choices for toppings: tomatoes, fresh basil, mushrooms, roasted peppers, red onion, chicken, and sun-dried tomatoes. Both goat and mozzarella cheese are low in fat.

2520 Cedar Springs Road
Dallas, TX 75201
214/871-1924

POLENTA PASTICCIATA CON SALSICCE

2 pounds polenta (corn meal)
8 cups water (divided use)
Salt to taste
2 pounds fresh tomato sauce made
with fresh Italian sausage,
(recipe follows)
2 cups grated Parmesan
2 cups bechamel (recipe follows)
1/2 pound buffalo mozzarella
Salt to taste

BECHAMEL
1/4 cup unsalted butter
1/4 cup flour
2 cups milk
Salt and ground white pepper

TOMATO SAUCE
1/4 cup extra-virgin olive oil
1/4 onion, minced
1/2 pound fresh Italian sausage,
cut into chunks
1 28-ounce can Italian plum tomatoes
or whole tomatoes, chopped
with juice
Salt
Ground pepper
Bay leaf
1 tablespoon chopped basil

Bring 5 cups water to a boil in a large saucepan (copper is best). Add salt. When the water reaches a boil, add polenta. With a wooden spoon, stir constantly until water is absorbed. Keep adding remaining 3 cups water until the polenta is cooked and the mixture does not stick to the sides of the pot.

Transfer the mixture to a wet marble cutting board and, with a knife that has been run under warm water, shape the dough into a mound. Let cool.

Grease a 10-by-16-inch pan with olive oil. Cut the polenta in 1/2-inch thick slices. Cover the bottom of the pan with polenta slices. Spoon the fresh tomato/sausage sauce on top. Sprinkle with Parmesan and spread a with little bechamel sauce. Add another layer of polenta making sure to cover all the spaces; follow with sauce, parmesan, and bechamel. Repeat the process two more times. Cover the last layer with a little tomato/sausage sauce, bechamel, Parmesan, and cubed mozzarella. Cook at 300 degrees for 15 minutes. Serve warm. Cut in squares with grated Parmesan as a garnish. *Serves 8.*

Bechamel - Melt the butter in a saucepan over low heat. Whisk in the flour stirring constantly for 5 minutes. Take the pan off the heat and whisk in the milk. Return it to the stove and cook over medium heat after it is well-blended. Keep stirring with a wooden spoon. Let it come to a boil then put the pot over simmering water and let it cook gently for another 10 to 15 minutes. Season accordingly.

Tomato Sauce - Heat the oil in a saucepan. Add the onion and sausage and cook over medium heat for 4 to 5 minutes. Add the tomatoes, salt, pepper and bay leaf. Heat to a boil. Simmer over low heat for 30 minutes, stirring frequently. Stir in the basil and simmer another 5 minutes. Strain the mixture through a colander into a bowl.

 Cut Parmesan cheese to one cup and vegetable oil to 2 tablespoons. Substitute skim milk and skim mozzarella cheese.

 Preston Barbera (California Red)
Ceretto Arneis (Italian White)

PAPA AL POMODORO

5 tablespoons extra-virgin olive oil
2 pounds ripe tomatoes, chopped
1/3 cup finely chopped onion
3 cloves garlic, minced
1 piece day-old Italian bread, chopped
3 tablespoons chopped fresh basil
  Salt and freshly ground pepper
  Basil leaves for garnish

Heat oil in a heavy skillet. Add tomatoes and onion, cook over medium-high heat about 10 minutes until soft. Stir in garlic. Add bread and stir until it softens and absorbs excess liquid. Remove from heat. Add chopped basil. Season to taste with salt and pepper. Garnish with basil leaves and serve at room temperature. *Serves 4.*

 Cut the olive oil to 1 tablespoon and fat calories are reduced to 32 percent.

 Anselmi Soave Classico Superiore (Italian White)
Pio Cesare Chardonnay (Italian White)

POMODORO CHEESECAKE

CRUST
1 1/2 cups graham cracker crumbs
2 tablespoons sugar
1/4 cup unsalted butter, melted

FILLING
16 ounces cream cheese, softened
2 eggs, lightly beaten
1/2 cup sugar
1 teaspoon vanilla extract
8 ounces sour cream

TOPPING
10 ounces frozen raspberries, thawed
1 tablespoon cornstarch

For crust, thoroughly combine graham cracker crumbs, sugar and melted butter. Press mixture into the bottom and sides of a greased 9-inch springform pan. Chill 15 to 30 minutes.

For filling, mix cream cheese, eggs, sugar, vanilla extract and sour cream. Beat with an electric mixer until smooth. Pour into the chilled crust, then bake in a preheated 375-degree oven for 25 minutes. Filling will be soft, but it will firm as it cools.

Cool cake on a wire rack to room temperature, then refrigerate for 8 hours or overnight.

For topping, strain juice from the thawed raspberries into a small saucepan. Set fruit aside. Add 1 tablespoon cornstarch to the fruit juice and stir until smooth, then cook over medium-low heat, stirring constantly, until bubbling and thickened. Remove from heat and gently stir in fruit. Cool, if necessary, then spread on chilled cake and return to refrigerator until topping is set.

Remove sides of pan before serving. *Serves 12-16.*

 S. Anderson Brut (California Sparkling)
Frescobaldi Brut (Italian Sparkling)

RISOTTO CON LASELLA DEL CONIGLIO

1/4 cup extra-virgin olive oil
1 onion, finely chopped
1 carrot, peeled and finely chopped
2 stalks celery, finely chopped
1 pound of rabbit meat, minced (2 1/2 to 3 pounds of rabbit will yield this, the butcher will trim the rabbit for you)
1/2 pound tomatoes, peeled, seeded and mashed
1/2 cup chopped nicoise olives
1 teaspoon oregano
2 cups dry white wine (Vernaccia)
3 cups arborio Italian rice
1 1/2 quarts chicken stock, preferably homemade
1/2 cup grated Parmesan
Salt and pepper to taste

Bring the stock to a simmer in a saucepan. Heat the olive oil in a heavy bottomed 3-quart saucepan and cook the onion, carrot and celery over medium heat stirring with a wooden spoon until the onion is golden brown (about 3 to 5 minutes). Add the minced rabbit meat and stir in the tomatoes, olives, oregano and white wine, a little at a time. Stir over medium heat for one minute. Add the rice and stir in order to coat the rice well.

Turn the heat to medium-high. Add about 1/2 cup of simmering stock to the rice and keep the mixture at a boil, stirring constantly. As soon as the stock is absorbed, add another 1/2 cup of stock and stir until it is absorbed. Continue adding stock 1/2 cup at a time, stirring constantly until the rice is creamy and tender. This process will take 20 to 30 minutes.

Remove the pan from the heat and stir in 1/2 cup of grated Parmesan. Taste and season with salt and pepper. Let cool for 2 minutes and serve immediately. *Serves 8 as an appetizer, or 6 as a main course.*

 This recipe falls below 30 percent fat calories. Fat could be further reduced by cutting back the oil and olives.

 Gaja Barbaresco (Italian Red)
Jaboulet-Vercherre Pouilly-Fuisse (French White)

FACING PAGE, from left:
Efisio and Lori Farris, Pomodoro and Arcodoro Bar;
Lori Finkelman Holben and David Holben, The Riviera

FOLLOWING PAGE, clockwise from left: Mario Reyes, 650 North;
Kevin Rathbun, Baby Routh; Annie Wong, Thai Taste;
Stephan Pyles, Routh Street Cafe

DUCK CANNELLONI
with Savoy Cabbage & Wild Mushrooms

ROASTED BREAST OF CHICKEN
with Goat Cheese, Basil and Truffle Vinaigrette served with Risotto Cakes

ROASTED TOMATO SOUP
with Crabmeat Croutons

Bon soir, les amis. The Riviera's owner, Franco Bertolasi, invites diners into the warm atmosphere of Southern France for a superb dining experience. Chefs Lori Finkelman Holben and David Holben create neo-classic cuisine that excites the diner's palate with exquisite tastes and textures.

David Holben predicts the team will continue to focus on its present cooking style. "We are going to stick with the Provencal approach. Our food has flavors that our customers are familiar with. It's food they want to have again and again."

The Riviera menu reflects flavors indigenous to Northern Italy and the South of France, as well as from the Holbens's French training. The Gnocchi Tartlets with Grilled Vegetables and Basil Cacciotta, Provencal Lobster Stew with Tomatoes,

Herbs and Rouille, and the Warm Quail Salad with Apples are light, fresh and healthy. The Holbens dub their style "food from the heart."

Lori Holben says, "I love food. Shopping at the Farmer's Market and just being around food is exhilarating. It's fun to learn what part the farmer plays and how certain vegetables grow."

The dynamic duo have studied and worked together for over twelve years. They agree that the most rewarding part of the job is seeing their customers satisfied. The Riviera has built a large family that includes chefs, staff and regular customers. Most of the staff have worked at the restaurant since its inception in 1984. "The first thing Lori does on a trip is buy presents for her co-workers," says David Holben.

Both attended the Culinary Institute of America and graduated in 1980 with high honors. The Holbens were selected for the coveted Mumm Cuvee Napa Award by Food & Wine magazine as two of the "Best New Chefs in America" in 1990. That same year D Magazine voted The Riviera the best restaurant in Dallas and Fort Worth.

The Holbens love Dallas and say their future is here. They anticipate with excitement new opportunites to play an even greater role in the Dallas cuisine scene.

LITEFARE

Foods are fresh and flavor is most important. Most menu items are prepared when ordered, so special requests are acceptable. Suggested meal: Sweet Garlic and Vegetable Soup, Sturgeon in Lobster-Saffron Broth (skip the fritter), and Fresh Fruit Sorbet.

7709 Inwood Road
Dallas, TX 75209
214/351-0094

DUCK CANNELLONI *with Savoy Cabbage & Wild Mushrooms*

DUCK CANNELLONI

- 5 duck legs
- 1 rib of celery, cut into medium dice
- 1 carrot, cut into medium dice
- 1 onion, cut into medium dice
- 5 parsley sprigs
- 5 cracked black peppercorns
- 1 pound mushrooms, finely chopped in food processor
- 4 shallots, finely chopped
- 2 tablespoons olive oil
- 1 cup grated Parmesan cheese (divided use)
- 2 tablespoons chopped fresh thyme
- 2 tablespoons olive oil
- 1 egg
  Salt and pepper to taste

SAVOY CABBAGE & WILD MUSHROOMS

- 4 pasta sheets, cooked and cut into 1 1/2 x 3-inch rectangles
- 1 head savoy cabbage, roughly cut into 1/2-inch pieces
- 8 ounces fresh wild mushrooms, cleaned and trimmed (shiitake, oyster, and portobello)
- 1/4 cup olive oil

GARNISH

- 1 red bell pepper, cut into fine julienne
- 1 yellow bell pepper, cut into fine julienne
- 1 tablespoon chopped chives

To cook duck legs, place in a large stockpot and cover with water. Bring to a boil and skim. After 1 hour, add vegetables, parsley and peppercorns. Cook another half hour, checking duck for tenderness. Remove from heat and cool. Remove legs and strain stock, reduce over medium heat by half until broth is intensely flavored. Pull duck meat from bones and chop. Set aside.

For duxelle, sweat mushrooms and shallots in a covered stockpot in olive oil over low heat until juices are released (about 10 to 15 minutes). Strain juices through a damp towel-lined strainer, pressing to squeeze all the juices out. Place mushroom liquid in a small saucepot and reduce until syrupy. Set aside. Transfer the mushroom solids to a mixing bowl. Add half the cheese, thyme, olive oil, egg and chopped duck meat. Season with salt and pepper.

To assemble cannelloni, lay pasta rectangles on a sheet pan. Sprinkle with Parmesan cheese and spoon a line of mushroom mixture down the center of each rectangle. Gently roll each into a tube and sprinkle tops with Parmesan. Place cannelloni on a parchment-lined sheet pan, and ladle a few ounces of duck broth on tray. Bake in 350-degree oven until hot (about 8 minutes).

Meanwhile, sweat savoy cabbage in olive oil. Add a few ounces of duck broth and simmer until tender. Season with salt and pepper, and keep warm. Saute wild mushrooms in olive oil. Season with salt and pepper, and keep warm.

For mushroom-duck broth, stir duck broth into mushroom liquid reduction. Season with salt and pepper.

To Assemble: Arrange savoy cabbage on warm plate. Place cannelloni in center of plates, scatter wild mushrooms, bell peppers and chives around plate and spoon broth around cannelloni. *Serves 6 to 8.*

 Beaucastel Chateauneuf du Pape (French Red)
Louis Jadot Clos Vougeot (French Red)

ROASTED BREAST OF CHICKEN
with Goat Cheese, Basil and Truffle Vinaigrette served with Risotto Cakes

8 split chicken breasts, bone-in,
   first joint attached
   Salt and pepper
2 tablespoons olive oil
24 whole basil leaves (divided use)
1 cup soft goat cheese (such as
   Montrachet)

TRUFFLE VINAIGRETTE
1 teaspoon Dijon mustard
2 tablespoons white wine vinegar
3 1/2 ounces extra-virgin olive oil
3 1/2 ounces truffle oil*
   Salt and pepper
   Chopped truffle (optional)

RISOTTO CAKES
2 shallots, minced
6 tablespoons butter (divided use)
2 1/2 cups arborio rice
6 cups chicken stock, simmering
   Few sprigs fresh thyme
4 eggs
8 ounces Parmesan cheese

***Available through Urbani Truffles, USA. Walnut oil is an acceptable substitute.**

Slip two basil leaves under the skin of each chicken breast. Season each breast with salt and pepper and sprinkle with olive oil. Roast in a preheated, 450-degree oven about 15 minutes or until just underdone. Remove from oven.

When the chicken has cooled slightly, remove rib bones. (Leave first joint attached.) With a small spoon, carefully slip goat cheese between the skin and meat of each breast, trying not to tear the crispy skin. Set aside and keep warm.

To prepare the vinaigrette, whisk mustard and vinegar together in a small bowl. Add the oils, salt and pepper, and truffle. Set aside.

To prepare risotto cakes, gently cook shallots in 4 tablespoons butter. Add rice, all at once, and stir well to break up lumps. Cook 2 to 3 minutes to coat all grains. Add a few ounces of simmering chicken stock and thyme. Cook over medium heat, stirring continuously. When the rice is almost dry, add a few more ounces of chicken stock. Repeat this process until rice is cooked. The grains should be al dente. Spread rice on a sheet pan to cool. When cool, stir in eggs and parmesan cheese and season with salt and pepper. Mix well and shape into 2-inch discs. These may be prepared up to 2 days in advance.

When ready to serve, return the filled chicken breasts to oven to crisp, heat and finish cooking. Saute risotto cakes in a small amount of butter, browning each side. When chicken is hot, arrange on warm plates, drizzle vinaigrette over breasts and serve with risotto cakes, and garnish with basil leaves. *Serves 8.*

 Omit sprinkling chicken breasts with olive oil. Remove skin before eating. Eliminate the vinaigrette dressing. To lower the fat calories of the risotto cakes, use 3 tablespoons butter, 4 ounces Parmesan cheese, substitute 2 whole eggs and 4 egg whites for the 4 eggs, and saute cakes in a non-stick pan.

 Chateau Ste. Michelle Semillon (Washington White)
Livio Felluga Pinot Grigio (Italian White)

ROASTED TOMATO SOUP *with Crab Meat Croutons*

1 quart meaty veal bones
5 large ripe tomatoes
2 slices smoked bacon, cut into small strips
1/2 stalk celery, cut into medium dice
2 onions, cut into medium dice
1 head garlic, split in half horizontally
2 1/2 ounces tomato paste
1 1/2 quarts quartered Roma tomatoes
3 quarts chicken stock
1 1/4 cups white wine
Fresh thyme sprigs
Bay leaves
Salt and pepper

GARNISH

1 pound lump crabmeat, cleaned of cartilage and shell
1/4 cup sun-dried tomatoes, coarsely chopped
1 teaspoon chopped rosemary
1 teaspoon chopped thyme
2 tablespoons olive oil
Lemon juice to taste
French bread for croutons

Roast the veal bones in hot oven until brown. Place tomatoes stem side down on a baking sheet and roast in 350-degree oven for 30 minutes.

In a hot casserole render the bacon. Add the celery and onions and lightly brown. Add the garlic and roasted veal bones. After about 5 minutes add the tomato paste and cook for another 10 minutes. Add roasted tomatoes, fresh Roma tomatoes, chicken stock and white wine. When it comes to a boil, skim, and add the herbs. Cook over low to medium heat about 3 hours or until the meat comes freely from the bone.

Remove the bones and puree the soup in the blender. Pass through a china cap or sieve. Season with salt and pepper.

For the garnish, mix the crab meat and the sun-dried tomatoes and bind with the herbs and olive oil. Add lemon juice, salt and pepper. Spoon onto a toasted crouton and float in the soup. *Yields 2 1/2 quarts, serves 10.*

 This soup is low fat if you start with a lean cut of veal, such as loin. Make the soup ahead so that you can defat the stock before blending.

 Merryvale Chardonnay (California White)
Villa Mt. Eden Zinfandel (California Red)

ROUTH STREET CAFE and BABY ROUTH

ROUTH STREET CAFE SHELLFISH PAN ROAST
with Guajillo Capellini Cakes

BABY ROUTH JALAPENO-SUNFLOWER CRUSTED CHICKEN

ROUTH STREET CAFE CHILLED SHRIMP & JICAMA SOUP
with Buttermilk & Basil

HOT BABY ROUTH

Routh Street Cafe is only ten years old and already considered a classic. The restaurant was selected in June 1992 as one of the top twenty-five restaurants in the United States by *Food & Wine* magazine. It matured early, because of the remarkable talents of chef and owner Stephan Pyles and partner John Dayton, who have educated native and national palates to Southwestern cuisine.

Pyles, born in Big Spring, Texas, combines classic training with his cutting edge creativity and unique blends of ingredients. These talents reflect his love of history and music, including opera. In 1991 Pyles won Top Southwest Chef at the first James Beard Awards. Earlier he was named to *Food & Wine* magazine's Honor Roll of American Chefs and each year he chairs the S.O.S. Taste of the Nation in Dallas.

When asked what direction his cuisine is now taking, Pyles replied, "My style is getting more rustic, heartier, with more aggressive flavor and different chilies. The food has been very subtle to accommodate our important wine list, and not overshadow the wines." Friends and customers will gain insight into Pyles's recipes when his book, *The New Texas Cuisine* comes out in March 1993.

Baby Routh was born just down the street five years ago in playful surroundings. Chef Kevin Rathbun has seven-and-a-half years of experience as executive sous chef at Commander's Palace in New Orleans and at Brennans in Houston. Food is a family affair for the Rathbuns. His mother is a pioneer maitre d' in Kansas City and his brother is also a chef.

Rathbun enjoys surprising patrons with delicious food combinations that represent the more relaxed style and atmosphere of Baby Routh. Rathbun says his innovative cuisine is inspired by ethnic restaurants and foods. "The continuing enjoyment regular customers express at my innovations encourages additional experimentation."

Baby Routh has the spirit of a child with crayons. Begin with a blank sheet and the food, artwork and people are the colors.

LITEFARE

Routh Street Cafe: This menu features grilled seafood, and interesting starches and vegetables. Try the Grilled Sturgeon on Annatto Rice or the Sea Scallops and Morel Relleno. Special requests are welcome.

Baby Routh: Asterisk items feature moderate portions of fish, with more starches and seasonings of vegetable, fruit or herb purees.

ROUTH STREET CAFE
3005 Routh Street
Dallas, TX 75201
214/871-7161

BABY ROUTH
2708 Routh Street
Dallas, TX 75201
214/871-2345

SHELLFISH PAN ROAST *with Guajillo Capellini Cakes*

1 cup dry white wine (more if needed)
12 clams, scrubbed
12 mussels, scrubbed and beards removed
12 medium shrimp
1/3 cup heavy cream
1 tablespoon diced celery
1 tablespoon diced red bell pepper
1 tablespoon diced onion
1 teaspoon chopped fresh basil
1/2 teaspoon Worcestershire sauce
1/2 teaspoon paprika
1 tablespoon homemade ketchup (or chili sauce)
1 tablespoon butter
Salt and white pepper to taste
6 Guajillo Capellini Cakes (recipe follows)

GUAJILLO CAPELLINI CAKES

8 ounces capellini (angel hair pasta), cooked al dente,drained, cooled and oiled
3 eggs, lightly beaten
1/4 cup half-and-half
1 tablespoon homemade ketchup (or chili sauce)
1 tablespoon roasted garlic puree
6 tablespoons guajillo chile paste (recipe follows)
4 tablespoons chopped fresh basil
1 1/2 cups grated pecorino cheese
Salt to taste
1/4 cup vegetable oil
1/4 cup olive oil

In a large saucepan, bring the wine to boil over high heat. Place the clams in the pan and cover with lid. Steam clams for about 2 minutes then add mussels. Cover pan and steam for 2 minutes longer or until shells have opened. Discard shells that do not open. Remove lid and add shrimp. Add more wine if all has evaporated. Cook uncovered until shrimp turn pink, about 30-45 seconds. Remove all seafood with a slotted spoon and keep in a warm place while finishing sauce.

Strain steaming broth and return to pan over high heat. Add cream, vegetables, basil, Worcestershire and paprika. Boil gently for 2 to 3 minutes. When thickened slightly, whisk in ketchup and butter and season with salt and white pepper.

Cook capellini cakes and place one on each of six plates. Arrange two of each of the shellfish around each capellini cake. Pour sauce over shellfish and serve. *Serves 6.*

Guajillo Capellini Cakes

Thoroughly combine eggs, half-and-half, ketchup, garlic puree, guajillo paste, basil and pecorino cheese. Add pasta and season with salt. Mix well. Form 12 small round cakes (or 6 large) from the mix.

Combine the oils in a large, heavy skillet and place over medium heat until lightly smoking. Add six of the capellini cakes and cook until golden brown on bottom (about 3 minutes). Flip cakes and cook an additional three minutes. Keep warm while cooking remaining cakes. *Makes 6 large or 12 small.*

Guajillo Chile Paste

Remove stems and seeds from 4 guajillo chilies. Lightly toast chilies on a flat griddle; be careful not to scorch. Cover with boiling water and let sit 10 to 15 minutes. Transfer chilies to blender and puree, adding just enough soaking liquid to make a paste.

 Handley Chardonnay (California White)

JALAPENO-SUNFLOWER CRUSTED CHICKEN

CRUST

- 4 jalapenos, seeded
- 1/8 cup cilantro, packed
- 1 cup all-purpose flour
- 1 cup sunflower seeds, unsalted
- 2 teaspoons salt
- 1/2 teaspoon black pepper

RELISH

- 2 tomatoes, peeled, seeded and diced
- 1 cinnamon stick
- 2 tablespoons Champagne vinegar
- 2 tablespoons sugar
- 1/2 teaspoon cracked pepper
- 1/2 teaspoon salt
- 1 tablespoon cilantro, chopped

ASIAGO CREAM FOR PASTA

- 3 cups heavy cream
- 3 shallots, sliced
- 2 garlic cloves, minced
- 1/2 cup Asiago cheese, grated*
- 10 ounces spinach pasta
- 1/4 cup diced tomatoes

PREPARING CHICKEN BREASTS

- 6 4-ounce chicken breasts, skinless and boneless
- 1/2 cup buttermilk
- 1/4 cup all-purpose flour
- Salt and pepper to taste

Grind jalapenos in food processor with cilantro until macerated. Add flour and sunflower seeds until blended. If mixture is too wet it will not crust; add 1/4 cup more flour if needed. Season with salt and pepper. Adjust seasoning if necessary.

Relish

Put all ingredients in a pot and bring to a boil. Remove from heat and let cool to room temperature. Serve in 1 hour.

Asiago Cream For Pasta

In a saucepan, put cream, shallot and garlic and reduce by 1/3. Add Asiago cheese and blend thoroughly.

* Asiago cheese is a semi-firm Italian cheese, and must age at least one year to be suitable for grating.

Chicken

Flour chicken breasts and dip in buttermilk, then in crust. Pack crust on. Saute in 350-degree oil on both sides. Finish in 350 degree oven for 4 minutes.

To assemble the plate, toss pasta with Asiago cream sauce, add diced tomatoes and toss again. Place chicken on bed of pasta. Spoon relish onto chicken. *Serves 6.*

 Substitute 3 cups half-and-half for cream in pasta to reduce fat calories to 36 percent. Eliminate salt and oil for sauteeing. Bake chicken in oven. Cut sunflower seeds to 1/2 cup.

 Franciscan Chardonnay (California White)
Bonny Doon Clos de Gilroy (California Red)

CHILLED SHRIMP & JICAMA SOUP *with Buttermilk & Basil*

3 cups jicama, peeled and diced
1 small cucumber, peeled, seeded and pureed
1/4 cup raspberry vinegar*
2 teaspoons granulated sugar
2 teaspoons salt (divided use)
8 ounces small shrimp, peeled and deveined
1/4 teaspoon cayenne pepper
2 tablespoons olive oil
2 cups buttermilk
1 cup heavy cream
1 cup sour cream
1/2 cup chopped fresh basil
1 red bell pepper, roasted, peeled and julienned
1 yellow bell pepper, roasted, peeled and julienned
Salt to taste

Place jicama and cucumber puree in a mixing bowl and mix with the vinegar, sugar and one teaspoon of the salt. Let stand while preparing shrimp.

In another bowl, place the shrimp and sprinkle with the remaining teaspoon of salt and the cayenne pepper.

Heat the olive oil in a skillet until lightly smoking. Add the shrimp and cook until they turn pink (about 2 minutes). Remove shrimp and set aside.

In a large bowl, combine the buttermilk and heavy cream, then whisk in the sour cream. Add the jicama-vinegar mix, the reserved shrimp, the basil and the roasted peppers. Combine thoroughly and taste. Season with salt if desired. *Serves 4 to 6.*

* Raspberry vinegar is available in specialty food stores.

Geyser Peak Semchard (California White)
Montevina Fume Blanc (California White)

HOT BABY ROUTH

6 tablespoons (3 ounces) Frangelico
6 tablespoons (3 ounces) Tuaca*
6 tablespoons (3 ounces) Amaretto
2 3/4 cups freshly brewed coffee
6 tablespoons (3 ounces) chocolate syrup
6 tablespoons caramel sauce
3/4 cup whipped cream
6 tablespoons peanuts, roasted and chopped
3/4 cup chocolate shavings

Gently warm the three liqueurs then add the coffee. Stir in the chocolate syrup.
Pour the mixture into heat resistant wine glasses. Drizzle 1 tablespoon of caramel sauce over each. Add a spoonful of cream and sprinkle tops with peanuts and chocolate shavings. *Makes eight 6-ounce servings.*

* Tuaca is an orange-vanilla flavored Italian liqueur available in liquor stores. You may substitute vanilla or orange extract, or one ounce Bouchant or Grand Marnier.

GRILLED MEDALLION OF SALMON
with Shrimp and a Roasted Corn Fondue

HERB CRUMBED FILLET OF ORANGE ROUGHY
with a Pineapple and Corn Ragout

TIRAMISU
with Sweet Basil Sauce

Mario Reyes comes to Plaza of the Americas Hotel from Canada, and the landmark five-star King Edward Hotel in Toronto. His unique award-winning style is featured in 650 North, the Plaza's signature restaurant.

Executive Chef Reyes brings an innovative and inspired cuisine to Dallas. "I love cooking! A few years ago I started creating my own things to define my style," says Reyes. He has traveled extensively, acquiring culinary skills that he plans to incorporate into the restaurant.

His stellar new menu features fish, beef and lamb with novel accompaniments and sauces. "I'm into a lot of salsa, ragout, compote, and coulis," says Reyes. The recipes he shares here are evidence of his lighter cooking style. Warm Lamb Tenderloin Salad Coated With Cashews and Raspberry Vinaigrette, Grilled Escalope of Chicken With a Trio of Peppers and Thai Noodles, and a selection of White Chocolate, Apricot or Coffee Gelato served in a Biscuit Basket, highlight the new menu.

Reyes is fanatic about fresh ingredients. Patrons can definitely count on the beauty of the food to match its taste. He is an artist as well as a chef. "I believe in detailed food, and its appearance is very important to me."

Designing meals for special occasions delights Reyes. He treats every party as an opportunity to express his self-acquired knowledge, while caring for every last detail.

Chef Reyes is a welcome addition to downtown dining. Expect his personality to shape the restaurant's tone and atmosphere. "I love dealing with the customers. 650 is not too casual or trendy, and is not an expensive place. Everything is moderately priced."

Reyes's move to Dallas represents the achievement of a personal goal: He has attained the position of Executive Chef before reaching age thirty. Look for exciting things from this young chef.

LITEFARE

Menu features fruits and vegetables in many interesting forms: salsas, ragouts, and compotes. Try the Herb Crumbed Fillet of Orange Roughy or Grilled Medallion of Salmon with Shrimp which are included here.

Plaza of the Americas Hotel
650 North Pearl Street
Dallas TX 75201
214/979-9000

GRILLED MEDALLION OF SALMON WITH SHRIMP
and a Roasted Corn Fondue

8 3-ounce Atlantic salmon fillets
1 pound shiitake mushrooms
1 pound French green beans (haricot vert)
1 cup fresh cranberries
2 tablespoons cooked black beans
24 medium shrimp, shelled and deveined
1 tablespoon olive oil (divided use)
2 tablespoons chopped chives for garnish

ROASTED CORN FONDUE
1/4 cup shallots, sliced
1 teaspoon olive oil
1 pound frozen corn
1 cup white wine
2 cups fish stock (recipe follows)
2 tablespoons heavy cream
Salt and pepper to taste

FISH STOCK
5 pounds fish bones
1/2 gallon water
8 ounces mirepoix* of leek, onion, celery
Bay leaf
Black peppercorns

Take a side of fresh Atlantic salmon and roll tightly into a log or tube shape. Roll in plastic wrap to help hold it together and cut into 1-inch thick medallions (about 3 ounces). Remove plastic wrap and put a toothpick through each medallion to hold it together during grilling. On a hot grill, mark the medallions of salmon nicely so you can see the marks. When grilling is complete, finish in oven for 2 minutes at 350 degrees.

Saute the shiitake mushrooms with French green beans, cranberries and black beans in 1/2 tablespoon olive oil. Then saute shrimp in remaining oil.

Place mushroom mixture at bottom of plate and top with a salmon medallion. Slowly spoon the fondue around plate, and place three shrimp on each plate. Garnish with chopped chives. *Serves 8.*

Roasted Corn Fondue
Saute the shallots in a medium saucepan with olive oil, then add the corn. Cook the corn until it is tender, then add white wine and reduce by half. Add fish stock and reduce by half again. Puree the mixture in a blender until it is the consistency of a sauce. Return to saucepan and bring to a boil over low heat, then add cream and seasoning to taste. Add a garnish of chopped chives when serving.

Fish stock
Boil water. Add bones. Drain and add mirepoix, bay leaf and peppercorns, then refill with water. Bring to a low boil and simmer 18 minutes. Strain through fine sieve.

* Mirepoix is roughly diced leek, onion and celery.

 This is a healthy, low-fat recipe if shrimp are boiled and mushrooms are sauteed in a non-stick pan or with cooking spray.

 St. Andrews Estate Bottled Chardonnay (California White)
Montevina Montanaro (California Red)

HERB CRUMBED FILLET OF ORANGE ROUGHY
with a Pineapple and Corn Ragout

8 4-ounce orange roughy fillets
1/4 cup olive oil (divided use)
   Salt and pepper to taste
2 tablespoons lime juice
2 tablespoons fresh rosemary, finely chopped
10 ounces fresh chervil, finely chopped
1 pound white bread crumbs
1 cup flour
3 eggs, lightly beaten
   Lemon wedges for garnish

PINEAPPLE AND CORN RAGOUT

1 ripe pineapple
2 tomatoes, diced, skin on
2/3 cup corn niblets (frozen or canned)
1 small red onion, diced
1 small clove garlic, minced
1/3 teaspoon chopped chives
1 teaspoon extra-virgin olive oil
3 tablespoons fresh lime juice
2 teaspoons honey
3 tablespoons soda water
   Salt and pepper to taste

Marinate fish with 3 tablespoons olive oil, salt, pepper and lime juice for 5 minutes. Mix the herbs with the bread crumbs. Coat fish first with flour, then eggs, and then pack on bread crumbs and set aside until ready to cook.

To cook, heat a heavy skillet and add one tablespoon olive oil. When the oil is hot, cook the coated fish for about 1 minute on each side until golden brown. Remove from skillet and finish in 375-degree oven for 6 to 8 minutes.

Pineapple and Corn Ragout
Just before serving, peel pineapple, quarter and trim off fibrous core. Dice and place in a bowl, add tomatoes, corn, onion, garlic, chives, olive oil, lime juice, honey, soda water and salt and pepper to taste. Makes approximately 8 cups.

Place Pineapple Ragout in the middle of a dinner plate. Arrange the fish fillet, overlapping the ragout. *Serves 8.*

 This is a low fat recipe if you use only 1 tablespoon olive oil for marinade. Saute fish in non-stick pan or use no-stick cooking spray. Another option is to oven-broil fish. Ragout would make a good accompaniment for other dishes.

 Hacienda Chenin Blanc (California White)
Chateau Souverain Sauvignon Blanc (California White)

TIRAMISU *with Sweet Basil Sauce*

1/2 cup heavy cream
6 eggs, separated
3/4 cup granulated sugar
1 pound mascarpone cheese
1/2 cup brandy
24 Italian Amaretti Biscuits or
Macaroons
1 1/2 cups strong espresso coffee
5 ounces semi-sweet chocolate,
shaved or finely chopped
Sweet basil sauce

SWEET BASIL SAUCE
1 quart heavy cream
8 ounces sugar
8 egg yolks, beaten
1 cup packed basil, roughly chopped,
pureed

Whip cream until firm, keep chilled. Beat egg whites until soft peaks form, gradually beat in sugar and continue beating until stiff. Refrigerate until ready to use.

In a large bowl beat egg yolks until fluffy, blend in mascarpone and brandy. Fold in egg whites, then whipped cream. Return to refrigerator.

Line the bottom of a shallow 10-inch serving bowl with 8 of the Amaretti biscuits and, using a brush, soak with espresso coffee. Spoon 1/3 of the mascarpone mixture on top. Sprinkle with 1/3 of the chocolate shavings. Repeat twice with the remaining ingredients. Refrigerate 6 to 8 hours before serving. *Serves 8.*

Sweet Basil Sauce
Bring cream and sugar to boil. Remove from heat. Cover and let sit in refrigerator for at least 4 hours or overnight.

Beat in egg yolks. Slowly beat in cream.

Bring back to a boil and add basil puree. Cook, stirring constantly, until mixture is thick enough to coat the back of a wooden spoon.

 Frangelico (Italian Hazelnut Liqueur)

YUM WOON SEN
(Hot and Spicy Glass Noodle, Shrimp and Chicken Salad)

PORK SATAY
with Peanut Sauce and Cucumber Salad

GAI YARNG
(Thai Barbecued Chicken)

CHICKEN COCONUT SOUP

"Sawasdee…" or "Hello" to those of you who do not speak Thai, says Annie Wong, the owner and chef of Thai Taste. She is saying "Hello" to many new friends through her traditional and creative Thai foods in the not-so-traditional-yet-creative old church Thai Taste occupies.

Wong was a home economics teacher at a convent in Bangkok when she decided to come to America in 1969. She discovered friendship in a foreign country by sharing her home cooking with new acquaintances. During her 22 years in the United States, her cooking style has gradually evolved from traditional Thai to its current mixture of Thai with American influences.

"I'm in love with New American cuisine and I use some of it with Thai food," Wong says. The menu of Thai Taste is comprised of traditional dishes Wong brought from her homeland, such as Eggplant Curry Thai Style, Panang (sliced meat with Thai red curry and coconut milk), and Sweet Rice with Coconut Milk and Fresh Mango.

Other dishes reflect her creativity and use of Southwestern foodstuffs as substitutes for certain Thai ingredients. Barbecued Game Hen, and Steamed Red Snapper Topped with Spicy Lime Sauce illustrate Wong's imaginative adaptations. This sometimes fiery food is good with Thai iced coffee or Thai Tea. If your taste leans toward wine, pick a sparkling wine, a Gewurztraminer or a Merlot or Zinfandel from the predominately Californian wine list.

The restaurant has a lunch menu of quick-to-prepare dishes for customers in a hurry. Dinner can be as relaxed as the diner desires.

Wong is as omnipresent as the stained glass (dated 1903) in the renovated church building. Customers seeking privacy may enjoy Wong's heavenly cuisine from a discreet table in the second-floor choir loft. The only time she jumps ship is during the Neiman Marcus Last Call sales which come around only twice a year.

LITEFARE

Thai cuisine uses coconut milk, which is high in saturated fat, and sauces that are high in sodium. Since food is mainly cooked to order, sodium can be lowered upon request. The Yum Woon Sen salad with 26 percent fat calories is an excellent choice. Choose steamed rice with entrees.

4501 Cole
Dallas, TX 75205
214/521-3513

YUM WOON SEN
(Hot and Spicy Glass Noodle, Shrimp and Chicken Salad)

8	ounces glass noodles*
3	tablespoons vegetable oil
1/4	cup dried shrimp*
1/2	cup boiled chicken strips
1/3	cup small shallots, sliced
1	medium red onion, thinly sliced
1/3	cup scallions, thinly sliced, green part only
2/3	cup small, tender inner leaves of celery
1/4	cup bean sprouts
1/4	cup carrots, cut julienne
1/3	cup fish sauce*
1/3	cup lemon juice
1 1/2	teaspoons sugar
4	teaspoons (or to taste) minced hot red chile peppers, such as cayenne, seeds removed (divided use)
12-16	cooked shrimp, peeled and deveined
1/2	cup cilantro leaves
	Lettuce

Soak glass noodles in cold water until tender to taste (about 30 minutes). Snip the noodles into 3 to 4 inch sections with scissors. Drain, rinse in cold water and drain again.

Heat 3 tablespoons of oil in a small pan. Fry the dried shrimp until just crisp. Drain and reserve.

Boil chicken strips in hot water until tender (about 5 minutes).

Combine shallots, onion, scallions, celery leaves, bean sprouts and carrots in a bowl; toss. Mix together fish sauce, lemon juice and sugar. Add to the bowl with the drained noodles, dried shrimp, chicken and one tablespoon minced chile or to taste.

Cut shrimp into thirds diagonally, reserving 4 whole for garnish. Toss and season with remaining chile, lemon juice and fish sauce to taste. Toss with cilantro leaves, julienned carrots and bean sprouts.

Arrange on a lettuce covered platter and garnish with the whole shrimp. Serve at room temperature. *Serves 4.*

* Glass noodles are white thin dried strands sold in oval skeins, like yarn. The noodles, dried shrimp and fish sauce are available at most Oriental markets.

 This is a good low-fat dish, but is high in sodium due to the fish sauce.

 Simi White Zinfandel (California Blush)
Beaulieu Johannisberg Riesling (California White)

PORK SATAY *with Peanut Sauce and Cucumber Salad*

1 pound boneless pork loin*
1 teaspoon curry powder
5 tablespoons coconut milk**
1 tablespoon garlic salt
1/2 teaspoon turmeric
 (or 2 drops yellow food color)
1 tablespoon sugar
1 tablespoon minced cilantro root
 (optional)
5 cloves crushed garlic
1/2 teaspoon black pepper
2 tablespoons vegetable oil
 Bamboo skewers, 6 inches long
 Cucumber salad (recipe follows)
 Peanut sauce (recipe follows)

PEANUT SAUCE
1 1/2 cups coconut milk or half-and-half
1 teaspoon red curry paste**
1 teaspoon paprika
1/2 cup chunky peanut butter
1 tablespoon white vinegar
1 tablespoon salad oil
2 tablespoon sugar
1 tablespoon salt

CUCUMBER SALAD
2 tablespoons warm water
3 tablespoons sugar
1/4 cup vinegar
1/4 teaspoon salt
1 cup thinly sliced cucumber
1/4 cup thinly sliced red onion
1 teaspoon thinly sliced fresh chile

Slice pork into strips one inch wide and 3 to 4 inches long. Place in a deep bowl. Add all other ingredients and stir together. Massage into meat gently for 5 minutes. Allow to marinate 2 hours.

Thread slices of pork on skewer. If pieces are small, put more than one on each skewer. Cook over charcoal grill or under broiler. Baste with coconut milk while cooking.

Turn and baste until done. Serve with peanut sauce and cucumber salad . *Serves 3 to 4.*

* Beef or chicken may be substituted for pork in this recipe.
** Canned coconut milk and red curry paste are available in Oriental markets.

Peanut Sauce
Heat coconut milk until boiling. Add red curry paste, paprika, peanut butter, vinegar, salad oil, sugar and salt. Stir continuously to keep from sticking to pan until well-mixed and evenly browned. Place in a flat dish for serving.

Cucumber Salad
Mix together and place in refrigerate until served.

 Coconut milk is very high in saturated fat. Choose lean, well-trimmed pork loin. Eliminate the 2 tablespoons oil and just taste the peanut sauce. Omit the added salt.

 Rutherford Hill Gewurztraminer (California White)
Benziger Chardonnay (California White)

GAI YARNG *(Thai Barbecued Chicken)*

  1 large chicken
  1 tablespoon sugar
  2 tablespoons minced cilantro root
10 cloves crushed garlic
  3 tablespoons fish sauce
1/4 teaspoon curry powder
  1 teaspoon black pepper
  1 tablespoon minced lemon grass*
1/2 cup coconut milk
    Sweet Chili Sauce*

Cut chicken into 4 pieces with sharp cleaver. Mix all ingredients except chicken and Sweet Chili Sauce in deep mixing bowl. Place chicken in bowl with other ingredients. Pierce chicken with knife and turn until completely coated. Let chicken marinate in sauce for at least 1 hour.

Place chicken on hot grill. Baste with remainder of sauce from bowl while cooking. Turn every 10 to 15 minutes. Grill until done. Serve with Sweet Chili Sauce. *Serves 4.*

* Lemon grass and Sweet Chili Sauce are available in most Oriental markets.

 Remove the skin before eating chicken to reduce the fat calories to 35 percent. Sodium is high due to fish sauce.

 Fall Creek Emerald Riesling (Texas White)
Saintsbury Garnet Pinot Noir (California Red)

CHICKEN COCONUT SOUP

1 cup sliced chicken breast
2 cups coconut milk
1 cup chicken broth
1 tablespoon sliced galangal root*
3 tablespoons fish sauce
3 tablespoons lemon or lime juice
1 tablespoon cayenne pepper
4 coriander leaves
4 makrut (wild lime) leaves*
6 dried chilies

Boil chicken in coconut milk and chicken broth until tender (about 5 minutes). Add sliced galangal root. Pour in serving dish and season with fish sauce and lemon juice to taste. Sprinkle with cayenne, coriander leaves and makrut leaves. Garnish with dried chilies before serving. *Serves 2.*

* Galangal root may be purchased at an Oriental market. Makrut leaves are optional.

 This soup is high in fat and sodium due to the coconut milk and fish sauce.

 Gloria Ferrer Carneros Cuvee (California Sparkling)
Fall Creek Chenin Blanc (Texas White)

RENIE STEVES

In her first book, *Dallas Is Cooking!* **Renie Steves** brings together friends, old and new, in an eclectic company of Dallas's finest chefs and their cuisine.

As owner of Cuisine Concepts, a food and wine consulting business in Fort Worth, Renie is constantly thinking of food and wine. This unique enterprise encompasses a cooking school, free-lance food and wine writing (with husband Sterling), food styling, and food and wine consultation for civic organizations, professional groups, private parties and restaurants. She began her teaching career in 1979 with The French Apron School of Cooking.

Renie is an International Association of Culinary Professionals Certified Culinary Professional (IACP) and has studied cooking under James Beard, Simone Beck, Gaston Lenotre, Giuliano Bugialli, Julia Child, Charles Finance, Marcella and Victor Hazan, Madeleine Kamman, Diana Kennedy, Jacques Pepin and others.

She is a member of Les Dames D'Escoffier, serves on the Dallas Chapter of the American Institute of Wine and Food board of directors, is a member of Les Amis du Vin, Les Amis D'Escoffier, Confrerie Saint Etienne Wine Society, Les Amis de Brouilly, Dallas Women's Wine Group, the IACP Foundation, is a recipient of the 1987 Domaine Chandon Rising Star Award, and was selected as one of Texas Top Twelve Tastemakers by Texas Homes in 1986.

She studied in the kitchens of Paul Bocuse in Lyon, Troisgros in Roanne, Paulo Preo at El Toula in Rome, Anton Mosimann at the Dorchester in London, and at Chez Augusta in Paris. Her love of cooking is second only to that for her family.

The Steves have three children, three grandchildren and two step-granddaughters. Sterling is a prominent Fort Worth trial lawyer, an avid fisherman and hunter, and sometimes goes hungry when Renie is working.

The Steves write Best Buys in Wine, a column in *The Fort Worth Star-Telegram*, a leisure column for Aura Magazine, and food, wine and travel articles for many other regional and national publications. They have been wine consultants for the Italian Trade Commission, and have judged

wine competitions from Dallas to Narbonne, France to Torgiano, Italy.

Renie's recipes have appeared in *Bon Appetit*, *Cooking Light*, the *San Francisco Chronicle*, the *Wine Spectator*, and many area publications. Future book projects include *Dallas Is Cooking Ethnic Cuisines*, and *Bistros, Bars, Grills, and Cafes, Fort Worth Is Cooking!*, and a cookbook of the recipes she has created throughout her career.

LINDA MCDONALD, MS, RD, LD

Linda McDonald, a dietitian and nutritionist, is dedicated to helping people eat healthy in all situations. Her nutrition tips in *Dallas is Cooking!* will demonstrate that food can be tasty and healthful.

Linda holds a Master's Degree from the University of Texas Graduate School of Biomedical Sciences. She is active in The American Dietetic Association, past chairman of the Consulting Nutritionists, and was honored by the American Heart Association for development of the first *Houston Area Dining Out Guide, Heart Healthy Houston.*

As a consultant to the restaurant and food industry, Linda's unique expertise has enhanced menus, food products, and educational materials. Her LiteFare and nutrition commentary have been popular features of the Houston Gourmet book series.

Linda and her husband, John, live in Houston, with two married children residing in Dallas and Detroit. Scott and Melissa McDonald are Dallas residents. Melissa's expertise and advice have been very beneficial in the development of *Dallas is Cooking!*

FRAN FAUNTLEROY

Fran Fauntleroy, owner of Houston Gourmet Publishing Company has published and sold over 100,000 copies of cookbooks and dining guides in Houston over the past 15 years.

Fran's first books, *Six Flew Over the Cuckoo's Kitchen* and its sequel, *Cuckoo, Too* were co-written with six lifelong friends. Her successful marketing of these books led to other cookbook marketing contracts and ultimately, the founding of Houston Gourmet Publishing.

As the last copies of one Houston Gourmet book are being sold, Fran is well into planning the next of the series. The Houston Gourmet books include three restaurant cookbooks and five menu guides, such as *Houston Gourmet 1991, Houston Gourmet '92, Cooks & Caterers,* and *Cooks 2.*

Fran is a wife and mother with three grown children and three grandchildren. She is a member of the Junior League of Houston, Kappa Kappa Gamma, and a regular tennis competitor at Houston Country Club.

WINE AND DINE *by Renie and Sterling Steves*

Is it fact or fiction? Is there really a relationship between food and wine? Definitely. With a few guidelines, even the novice can select the perfect wine to go with fish.

Food and wine can bring out the best or the worst qualities in one another; however, there are no absolute rules that declare an individual right or wrong when tasting because each person has a different threshold for acid, sugar, and various flavors such as herbs and spices.

A few ground rules are helpful in understanding where to start. To see if a food is 'wine friendly,' take a sip of wine and then a bite of food, and another sip of wine. Think about the acid or balance, the texture in the mouth, the weight or body of the food and wine, and the flavors - from sweet, tart, or herbaceous, to pleasing or not pleasing. Is the aftertaste pleasant? If harmony results, the taster is anxious to try the same combination again.

Selection begins with understanding the basic qualities of the main wine varietals. For whites, Chardonnay can be either light, medium or heavy in body. It is often described as appley, lemony, creamy or vanillin.

The styles of Sauvignon Blanc may be grassy, herbaceous, or grapefruity. Chenin Blanc is fruity, melon-like, pineapply or lemony; it is often slightly sweet, but is also made in a dry style. Johannisberg Riesling is fruity and floral, usually full of apricots, peaches and green apples. Gewurztraminer stands alone in its distinct spiciness with geranium and grapefruit accents.

White wines taste better when cool but not too chilled. The ice bucket that arrives at the restaurant table keeps the wine too cold to enjoy the flavors and nuances of a good wine.

As for the reds, if they are young and heavily oaked, the tannins may be rough and coarse. As the wine ages, the tannins become softer and smoother. Cabernet Sauvignon is often described with the words currants, green bell pepper, mint, herbs or tea. Merlot has these same descriptors in softer forms, plus floral, cedar and cherry. Burgundy's red grape, Pinot Noir, smells of berries and earth. Its style may be light and fruity, full of

violets, or rich and earthy, enhanced with wild mushrooms. California's own grape varietal, Zinfandel, erupts with eucalyptus, cedar, and jamminess if it is heavy. A light Zinfandel has blackberry, cherry and herbs and spices upfront.

Sparkling wine or Champagne can be served throughout the meal if your personal taste desires. A light one can be served with a light dish such as a cold fish pate or ham, or a heavy Champagne or sparkler with a game dish, roast pork or sausage.

> *"To see if a food is wine friendly, sip the wine and then taste the food."*

Care must be taken when offering a sparkling wine with dessert. The dessert should never be sweeter than the wine. Fruit tarts and cheesecake are best, but never chocolate.

The body or density of the food should match the density or flavor strength of the wine. An easy way to remember this is to match delicate food to delicate wine, and strong food to strong wine. A spicy or forward food, such as Thai or Southwestern, is complemented by a wine that has spice in its taste, such as a Gewurztraminer. If the dish needs a red wine, try a Zinfandel which also offers a gusty spiciness.

The lightness of poached sole would not be overshadowed by light Sauvignon Blanc, but a salmon steak, because of its heavier fatty consistency, accepts a light red such as a Beaujolais and Pinot Noirs. The tannins in a Cabernet Sauvignon, from the residue of the barrel oak and grape stems, would overpower the salmon. Tannins can make your teeth feel like they have a wool blanket over them. Moderate tannins give a pleasing astringency that goes well with beef, venison, and duck.

Matching the food and wine by virtue of similar flavors is another valid route. Chicken roasted with herbs would meld perfectly with an herbaceous wine such as Sauvignon Blanc. An earthy Pinot Noir would echo the earthiness of a veal chop with wild mushrooms. The herb and mint overtones traditionally found in Cabernet Sauvignon elegantly compliment lamb flavored with rosemary and mint. It is helpful for the cook to know, when in doubt, to use a wine in the preparation of the dish, and drink the same wine with it. When cooking with wine, it is often reduced to make a more

concentrated taste. The wine must be good to start with or undesirable flavors will be accentuated.

When in doubt about choosing a wine, think about the ingredients and their origin. It is a safe bet to serve Italian wine with Italian food or Spanish wine with Spanish food.

Poultry, pork and veal are the chameleons of food. The choice of wine is totally guided by the way in which the dish is prepared, its ingredients and the sauce. Taste, texture, and appearance can all change dramatically. Sauteeing is usually dependent on butter, onions, lemon and herbs. Choose a high acid white wine, a Chardonnay or Sauvignon Blanc, to balance the flavors of any of these meats. If the meat is marinated in peppers, garlic, ginger and soy and then smoked, a wine with slight sweetness, a Chenin Blanc, Johannisberg Riesling or Gewurztraminer, is best to meld the spicy and smoky flavors.

Grilling adds pungent flavor, so grilled poultry, pork, or veal will be complimented by a fairly light red such as a single vineyard Beaujolais or Cotes du Rhone. If the dish has ricotta and parmesan topping surrounded by a tomato mint sauce,

the wine should be elevated to a richer Cabernet Sauvignon or Italian Barolo.

Traditions and folklore are an important part of matching wine to food. There are certain wines that have been served with certain food for decades. Many of these are local wines paired with local foods — Roquefort and Sauternes, escargot and Burgundy, sausage and Riesling, lamb and Bordeaux, stilton and Port. Certain pairings have become naturals — pecans and Cabernet, red bell pepper and Sauvignon Blanc, tomatoes and Zinfandel, orange, tarragon or apple with Chardonnay, Spanish tapas with Fino (Sherry), smoked fish and Gewurztraminer, and creamy pasta with a young fruity Chianti.

Remember, the best food wines are those of nuance, complexity, flavor and balance. Of course, those are always the best wines anyway.

HEALTHY EATING GUIDLINES *by Linda McDonald, M.S.,R.D.,L.D.*

The secret to healthy eating is to enjoy foods that taste good and are good for you. No food or recipe is "good" or "bad". What you do with food or a recipe may be beneficial or harmful. Smart eating is understanding food and learning how to use basic principles of balance and moderation.

The LiteFare tips, recipe modifications and nutrition information will help you make informed choices. Use the nutrient analysis chart to check the difference between the original recipe and the modified version. Then use the suggested modifications based on your particular health needs and your eating plans for the rest of the day. Remember that balance and moderation are the keys to eating healthy.

RECIPE MODIFICATIONS

Recipe modifications change one or more of the ingredients to make the outcome more beneficial. The four basic reasons for modifying recipes are:

- To reduce fat and cholesterol.
- To reduce sodium.
- To reduce sugar.
- To add fiber.

A recipe can be modified in four ways:

- Eliminate an ingredient.
- Change the amount of an ingredient.
- Substitute one ingredient for another.
- Change the cooking method.

TO REDUCE FAT & CHOLESTEROL:

Limit the portion of meat, fish or poultry to 3 to 4 ounces per serving. The current dietary recommendations are to eat no more than 6 ounces of lean meat, poultry or fish per day.

Choose lean cuts of meat and trim all visible fat before cooking. This includes removing the skin of poultry, which can be done before or after cooking. If you are using a moist cooking method (stewing, boiling, covered casserole), remove the skin before cooking. If using a dry cooking method (baking, broiling, grilling), leave the skin on during cooking to keep the product from drying out, but remove the skin before eating.

Plan a variety of proteins - animal and vegetable. Cycle red meat, poultry, and fish with dried beans, peas and lentils.

Marinating lean cuts of meat tenderizes them by breaking down muscle fiber. This is done by the acid part of the marinade - vinegar, wine, pineapple juice, etc. Oil is not necessary. Prick the meat all over with a fork to allow the marinade to penetrate thoroughly.

Use non-fat or 1 percent dairy products. Replace whole milk cheese with cheese made from skim milk, such as part-skim milk mozzarella. Try some of the new low-fat cheeses.

Prepared meats and cheeses should have no more than 5 grams of fat per ounce. Check the labels or ask the grocer where you shop.

Use sharp cheddar and other strong flavored cheeses. Place cheese on top to have the greatest influence on your taste buds.

Low-fat cooking methods include broiling, baking, roasting, poaching, and stir-frying. Utensils for low fat cooking are non-stick cookware, vegetable cooking spray, and steamers.

Saute with broth, wine or water instead of oils and butter.

Microwave vegetables in a covered dish with just a small amount of water, rather than sauteeing in oil or butter.

Make soups, sauces, stocks, and stews ahead of time. Chill, then remove all hardened fat from the top. If you don't have time to do this, skim off as much fat as possible, then add several ice cubes. The fat will congeal and cling to the ice cubes, which can be discarded.

If you can't make your own stocks, look for low-fat and low-sodium canned beef or chicken broth. Be sure to defat canned broth by chilling and skimming off hardened fat.

Use fewer egg yolks and whole eggs in cooking. Substitute two egg whites for each whole egg.

Use eggless pasta in place of egg pastas. Most dry pastas are eggless, and most fresh pastas use eggs, but check the ingredient labels.

Use nuts, seeds, olives, cheese, butter, margarine, and oils in moderation.

Olive and canola oils are the best choices for cooking. Use olive oil for sauteeing and salad dressings, choose canola for baking.

Try the following low-fat substitutions:

Cream
1/3 cup non-fat dry milk in 1 cup skim milk or canned evaporated skim milk.

Sour Cream
Non-fat yogurt or 1 cup non-fat or 1% cottage cheese + 1 tablespoon lemon juice, blended.

Mayonnaise
1 cup plain non-fat yogurt and 1/2 cup light mayonnaise.

Various starches can be used to thicken soup broths after substituting skim or low-fat milk for cream. Cornstarch will thicken a liquid without making it cloudy the way flour does. For 2 cups broth, mix 1 tablespoon starch or flour with 2 tablespoons cold water and stir the mixture until smooth. Add 2 tablespoons of the hot broth and stir the mixture again. Then gradually add the cornstarch mixture to the liquid you wish to thicken. Cook, stirring, for several minutes or until desired thickness is reached.

TO REDUCE SODIUM:

Salt is an acquired taste. Your desire for salt will diminish as you gradually reduce the amount you use. You will begin to enjoy the taste of the food rather than the salt.

Add salt last, after tasting the food. Use just enough to correct food's flavor. Remove the salt shaker from the table.

Nothing else tastes exactly like salt, but other seasonings can enhance the flavor of foods and compensate for the salt you eliminate. Use the following seasonings to add zest to foods:

Lemon or Lime Juice - use on salads and cooked vegetables. For more juice, microwave fruit for 30-60 seconds before juicing.

Citrus Zest - the thin outer layer of an orange, lemon or other citrus peel. Adds flavor to baked goods, sauces and other dishes. Use a zester or grater.

Flavored Vinegars - (tarragon, raspberry, wine)

Dried Onion Flakes, Onion or Garlic Powder, Garlic Cloves

Condiments - Worcestershire sauce, hot pepper sauce, mustard, soy, etc. are relatively high in sodium. If used sparingly, they can enliven foods without overdoing the sodium.

Herbs - Fresh herbs have the best flavor. If unavailable, substitute 1/2 to 1 teaspoon dried herb per tablespoon of fresh herb. Crush the dried herb to release its flavor.

Wines & Liqueurs - The alcohol evaporates if cooked at or above boiling temperature, eliminating most of the alcohol and calories while the flavor remains.

Salt can be eliminated or reduced in all recipes except yeast breads, where salt is necessary to control the growth of the yeast. Even in yeast breads, salt can usually be reduced to one teaspoon per tablespoon of dry yeast.

Use salt-free or low-sodium canned products. Rinse canned products such as beans with water before using.

Salt is not necessary in the boiling water when cooking pasta, rice, and other grains.

TO REDUCE SUGAR:

Sugar can be reduced by one-third to one-half in most recipes. In cookies, bars, and cakes replace the sugar you have eliminated with non-fat dry milk.

Brown sugar and honey are sweeter than sugar, and can be substituted for white sugar using a considerably smaller amount. Nutritionally they are the same, so there is no advantage to brown sugar or honey.

Flavor can be enhanced with spices (cinnamon, nutmeg or allspice) and extracts (vanilla, almond, orange or lemon). Doubling the amount of vanilla a recipe calls for will increase the sweetness without adding calories.

When reducing sugar in a recipe, substitute fruit juice for the liquid or add fruits such as raisins, dried apricots, dates or bananas. Frozen orange or apple juice concentrate can be added.

1 tablespoon concentrate = 1/4 cup fresh juice.

TO ADD FIBER:

Use more whole grains (bulghur, brown rice, corn, barley and oatmeal), vegetables, dried beans, split peas and lentils.

Substitute whole-wheat flour for white flour whenever possible. It is heavier than white flour, so use less; 7/8 cup whole wheat flour for one cup white flour. Some recipes do well with all whole-wheat flour, others are better when half whole-wheat and half white flour is used.

Add wheat bran, oat bran, oatmeal or farina to baked products, cereals, casseroles, and soups. Start with one or two tablespoons and increase gradually. Substitute up to 1/2 cup oatmeal or oat bran for part of the flour in baked goods.

Use unpeeled potatoes whenever possible in soups, stews or for oven fries.

Use whole grain pastas and brown or wild rice.

NUTRITIONAL ANALYSIS
Health Conscious Recipes

	Portion	Calories	Protein (g)	Carbohydrates (g)	Fat (g)	% Fat Calories	Cholesterol (mg)	Sodium (mg)**	Dietary Fiber (g)
Actuelle Summer Salad (Actuelle)	1/8 recipe	140	5	18	8	43	0	63	1.5
* Modified Version	1/8 recipe	110	5	18	4	29	0	63	1.5
Adriatic Shrimp Soup (Gaspar's)	1 serving	92	7	6	4	41	43	538	1
* Modified Version	1 serving	62	7	6	1	13	43	538	1
Baked Coho Salmon Roulades(Cafe Margaux)	1 serving	333	27	12	19	52	111	385	1
* Modified Version	1 serving	218	27	12	6	26	80	269	1
Banana Nut Ravioli with Vanilla Bean Sauce (Dakota's)	1 serving	814	7	55	65	70	223	118	1.5
Beef Tenderloin/Crust/Sauce (Gaspar's)	8 ounces	1098	50	44	80	65	282	701	4
* Modified Version	4 ounces	579	42	47	24	37	129	477	4
* Black Bean Soup (Javier's)	1 serving	141	7	21	4	22	0	5	4
Braised Lamb Shank/Polenta (The Grape)	1 serving	733	54	34	42	52	190	495	6
* Modified Version	1 serving	518	60	34	16	28	188	499	6
Brazos Ancho Fudge Pie (Brazos)	1 slice	777	8	74	55	60	128	328	1
Brazos Turkey Chili (Brazos)	1/8 recipe	352	20	21	23	55	42	435	4
* Modified Version	1/8 recipe	264	26	21	10	32	50	430	4
Carpaccio/Peppercorn Dressing (Actuelle)	1/8 recipe	378	17	2	33	80	47	302	0
Chesapeake Oyster Stew (The Conservatory)	1 serving	819	22	69	52	57	146	999	3
* Modified Version	1 serving	696	22	69	37	48	104	1016	3
Chicken Bombay Sandwich (Lady Primrose's)	1 sandwich	384	19	27	23	53	46	637	3
* Modified Version	1 sandwich	299	19	27	14	38	44	449	3
Chicken Coconut Soup (Thai Taste)	1 serving	610	15	16	58	81	23	1605	0
Chilled Shrimp & Jicama Soup (Routh St. Cafe)	1/6 recipe	406	12	26	28	62	132	908	1
Cioppino (Cafe Pacific)	1 serving	578	33	9	43	66	113	913	2
* Modified Version	1 serving	280	33	9	9	29	113	913	2
Crab Cakes (Crockett's)	1 serving	240	12	12	16	59	83	333	0.5
Crab Cakes (Dakota's)	1 cake	74	8	1	4	51	45	243	0
* Modified Version	1 cake	57	8	1	2	34	176	223	0
Crab Cakes/Chutney/Sauce (The Grape)	1 serving	762	14	21	70	81	220	856	2
* Modified Version	1 serving	232	13	18	12	48	62	293	2
* Crookneck Squash/Tomato Soup(Crockett's)	1 serving	92	4	16	2	19	0	309	1
* Crowned Pork Loin/Sauce (The French Room)	6 ounces	402	40	28	11	25	121	281	2
Dakota's Caesar Dressing (Dakota's)	1 Tablespoon	90	1	0	10	97	9	71	0
Dancing Tasmanian Lobster (Avner's)	1 serving	330	32	15	16	44	125	1306	3
* Modified Version	1 serving	255	32	15	8	27	117	1277	3
Duck Cannelloni (The Riviera)	1/8 recipe	465	18	29	31	60	89	282	3
* Fraises Au Poivre Noir (Cafe Pacific)	1 serving	102	1	17	1	5	0	2	4
Gai Yarng (Thai Taste)	1 serving	820	93	7	44	50	275	1635	0
* Modified Version	1 serving	654	93	7	26	35	243	1635	0
Green Sauce (Javier's)	1 cup	58	1	6	4	56	0	389	1.5
* Modified Version	1 cup	28	1	6	1	16	0	389	1.5
* Grilled Chicken Breast/Sauce(Crockett's)	1 serving	386	39	38	9	20	78	298	1
* Grilled Curried Venison with Apricots And Tasso (Actuelle)	1/8 recipe	427	31	42	11	23	17	1109	4
Grilled Florida Grouper (The Conservatory)	1 serving	610	42	22	40	58	86	390	3
* Modified Version	1 serving	299	39	6	12	38	73	359	2

**Sodium content includes only salt in recipes with specific amounts.

NUTRITIONAL ANALYSIS
Health Conscious Recipes

	Portion	Calories	Protein (g)	Carbohydrates (g)	Fat (g)	% Fat Calories	Cholesterol (mg)	Sodium (mg)**	Dietary Fiber(g)
Grilled Lamb Chops Provençal (City Cafe)	4 chops	710	64	1	48	62	209	424	0
* Modified Version	2 chops	355	32	1	24	62	104	123	0
* Grilled Medallion of Salmon(650 North)	1 serving	277	26	22	10	30	96	103	3
Grilled Pork Loin/Sauce (City Cafe)	8 ounces	319	50	7	9	26	161	338	0
* Modified Version	5 ounces	211	31	7	6	25	101	294	0
Herb Fillet of Orange Roughy (650 North)	1 serving	565	30	72	21	31	103	408	4
* Modified Version	1 serving	519	30	72	15	25	103	408	4
Hot Baby Routh	1 serving	314	28	4	19	49	31	52	2
Insalata di Carciofi (Mi Piaci)	1 serving	399	20	25	25	56	30	712	3
* Modified Version	1 serving	195	9	24	7	33	10	247	3
Jalapeno-Sunflower Chicken (Routh Street Cafe)	1 serving	1205	58	78	74	55	327	1029	2
* Modified Version	1 serving	802	57	77	28	32	209	322	1.5
Juniper Roast Chicken	1/4 recipe	449	43	3	27	54	140	386	0
* Modified Version	1/4 recipe	359	43	6	16	41	140	386	0
Juniper Roquefort Cheese Potatoes	1/4 recipe	909	24	41	73	72	237	1286	2
Kahlua Creme Caramel (The Grape)	1 serving	818	14	78	50	54	576	159	0
* Lemon Gelato (Mi Piaci)	1 cup	282	1	59	7	22	27	8	0
Linguini Verde (Cafe Pacific)	1 entre	931	16	67	70	66	150	220	4
* Modified Version	1 entre	466	14	65	19	35	57	210	4
Lobster Salad/Mangoes (The French Room)	1 serving	507	46	36	21	36	146	615	4
* Modified Version	1 serving	477	46	36	17	33	146	615	4
Lobster Yellow Tomato Bisque with Lobster Pico de Gallo (Nana Grill)	1 serving	925	8	27	91	85	295	115	4
Lousiana Crawfish/Grits (Cafe Margaux)	1 entre	585	39	14	41	64	369	592	2
Main Street Spanish Garlic Soup/Aioli	1 cup	236	7	24	11	38	0	482	0.5
* Modified Version	1 cup	206	7	24	7	30	0	482	0.5
Medallions de Veau au Citron Vert (Juniper)	1 serving	342	32	6	21	56	139	409	0
* Modified Version	1 serving	252	32	6	11	40	124	351	0
* Mother Hubbard's Squash Soup (Lady Primrose's)	1 serving	161	6	27	5	25	11	266	0.5
Osso Buco Milanese (Mi Piaci)	1 serving	1677	97	121	87	47	424	1687	2
* Modified Version	1 serving	1281	92	120	44	32	310	661	2
Oriental Glazed Roast Quail (City Cafe)	1 serving	1056	45	152	30	25	0	535	1.5
* Modified Version	1 serving	882	42	152	12	12	0	513	1.5
Pan-Fried Brussels Sprouts (The French Room)	1 serving	157	6	16	10	50	2	372	3
* Modified Version	1 serving	111	4	15	5	36	1	196	3
Pappa al Pomodoro	1 serving	229	3	17	18	66	0	59	3
* Modified Version	1 serving	110	3	17	4	32	0	59	3
Pear Cake With Cream Cheese Icing(Crockett's)	1 slice	558	6	72	29	45	130	146	2
Pear & Stilton Sandwich (Lady Primrose's)	1 serving	328	12	32	14	38	39	872	4
* Modified Version	1 serving	275	9	32	10	32	26	616	4
Polenta Pasticciata (Pomodoro)	1 serving	885	36	100	40	40	83	1263	8
* Modified Version	1 serving	819	32	102	33	35	74	1061	8
Pomodoro Cheesecake	1/16 recipe	298	5	29	18	54	72	230	1.5
Pork Satay with Peanut Sauce and Cucumber Salad (Thai Taste)	1/4 recipe	761	36	36	56	64	81	3503	2.5
Potato Crusted Black Sea Bass (Gaspar's)	1 serving	566	27	34	36	56	168	356	4
* Modified Version	1 serving	340	28	35	9	25	78	243	4

**Sodium content includes only salt in recipes with specific amounts.

NUTRITIONAL ANALYSIS
Health Conscious Recipes

	Portion	Calories	Protein (g)	Carbohydrates (g)	Fat (g)	% Fat Calories	Cholesterol (mg)	Sodium (mg)**	Dietary Fiber(g)
* Potato-Green Chile Soup (City Cafe)	1 serving	179	6	32	2	12	0	584	2
* Red Sauce (Javier's)	1 cup	32	1	7	0	7	0	130	0.5
Red Snapper a la Javier (Javier's)	1 serving	260	33	8	11	37	55	347	2
* Modified Version	1 serving	230	33	8	7	29	55	347	2
Red Snapper & Salmon Tartare (Actuelle)	1/8 recipe	223	15	18	10	40	28	476	1
* Modified Version	1/8 recipe	179	14	18	5	26	17	402	1
* Risotto con Lasella del Coniglio (Pomodoro)	1 entre	608	29	79	17	26	49	803	2
Roasted Breast of Chicken (The Riviera)	1 serving	1209	88	49	71	54	349	738	3
* Modified Version	1 serving	884	64	48	40	40	126	738	3
* Roasted Tomato Soup (The Riviera)	1 serving	281	22	32	7	23	64	1038	4
* Saffron Risotto (Mi Piaci)	1 serving	722	26	100	23	29	58	148	4
Salmone Al Salmoriglio (Mi Piaci)	1 serving	421	28	0	34	73	36	2279	0
* Modified Version	1 serving	182	28	0	7	34	36	1213	0
Scotch Eggs (Lady Primrose's)	1 egg	451	30	25	25	51	427	1010	1
* Modified Version	1 egg	416	46	27	12	28	267	850	1
She Crab Soup (Nana Grill)	1 serving	358	10	20	26	64	160	707	0
Shellfish Pan Roast with Guajillo Capellini Cakes (Routh Street Cafe)	1 serving	576	25	30	38	59	206	664	0
Shepherd's Pie (Lady Primrose's)	1 serving	514	26	43	27	47	93	471	1
* Modified Version	1 serving	499	26	43	25	45	90	500	1
Shrimp Pacific (Cafe Pacific)	1 serving	647	14	10	62	84	296	598	1
Shrimp with Carrot Juice and Thai Spices (Gaspar's)	1 serving	160	6	15	9	49	66	182	4
* Modified Version	1 serving	85	6	15	1	5	43	95	4
Spicy Peanut Sauce (Dakota's)	1/4 cup	127	4	8	10	64	0	295	1
Steamed Sea Scallops/Sauce (Avner's)	1 serving	325	30	28	12	31	68	1426	4
* Modified Version	1 serving	275	30	28	6	19	68	1426	4
Swordfish/Marinated Peppers (Nana Grill)	1 serving	794	45	23	59	66	85	640	2
* Modified Version	1 serving	358	44	17	12	31	85	371	2
Thornbury Castle Sponge with Walnut Toffee Sauce (Lady Primrose's)	1 slice	374	5	54	17	39	74	417	3
Tikka Spiced Chicken/Lentils (Avner's)	1 serving	1202	108	62	58	43	265	994	13
* Modified Version	1 serving	725	68	62	24	29	133	876	13
Tiramisu with Sweet Basil Sauce (650 North)	1 serving	1222	21	99	83	59	585	184	1
Toasted Pumpkin Seed Salsa (Dakota's)	1/4 cup	53	2	6	3	48	0	410	1.5
* Modified Version	1/4 cup	33	1	5	1	30	0	20	1.5
Tortilla Salad/Bean Cakes (The Conservatory)	1 serving	644	19	76	32	42	13	825	6
* Modified Version	1 serving	361	17	55	11	25	13	173	6
* Tortilla Soup (Crockett's)	1 serving	117	6	20	3	19	1	952	3
Vegetable Tart Niçoise (Juniper)	1/8 recipe	271	9	20	20	61	7	332	3
* Modified Version	1/8 recipe	207	9	20	12	49	7	312	3
Venison Sausage Quesadillas (Dakota's)	1 serving	586	26	36	37	57	77	661	1.5
* Modified Version	1 serving	354	26	36	12	30	54	170	1.5
White Chocolate Mousse (Cafe Pacific)	1 serving	427	6	23	40	75	188	34	0
* Whole-wheat Angel Hair Pasta (Crockett's)	1 serving	320	14	42	11	29	89	165	1
* Yum Woon Sen (Thai Taste)	1 serving	372	8	62	11	26	38	2039	2

**Sodium content includes only salt in recipes with specific amounts.

INDEX

WHO'S WHO

Key To Back Cover Photograph

1 **Efisio Farris**, *Pomodoro and Arcodoro Bar*
2 **Salvadore Gisellu**, *Pomodoro and Arcodoro Bar*
3 **Nancy Beckham**, *Brazos and Main Street News*
4 **Clive O'Donoghue**, *Actuelle*
5 **Karl Brandmeir**, *Crockett's*
6 **Vivian Young**, *Lady Primrose's*
7 **Mario Reyes**, *650 North*
8 **Ron Rosenbaum**, *Nana Grill*
9 **James Severson**, *Dakota's*
10 **Renie Steves**, *Author*
11 **Mark Davis**, *Photographer*
12 **Amy Samuel**, *Avner's*
13 **Lori Finkelman Holben**, *The Riviera*
14 **Annie Wong**, *Thai Taste*
15 **Fran Fauntleroy**, *Publisher*
16 **Alicia Bradshaw**, *Editorial Assistant*
17 **Kevin Rathbun**, *Baby Routh*
18 **Christian Gerber**, *Juniper*
19 **Jim Mills**, *The Conservatory and Beau Nash*
20 **Charlotte Parker**, *The Grape*
21 **Kathy McDaniel**, *The Grape*
22 **David Holben**, *The Riviera*
23 **Kay Agnew**, *Cafe Margaux*
24 **Stephan Pyles**, *Routh Street Cafe*

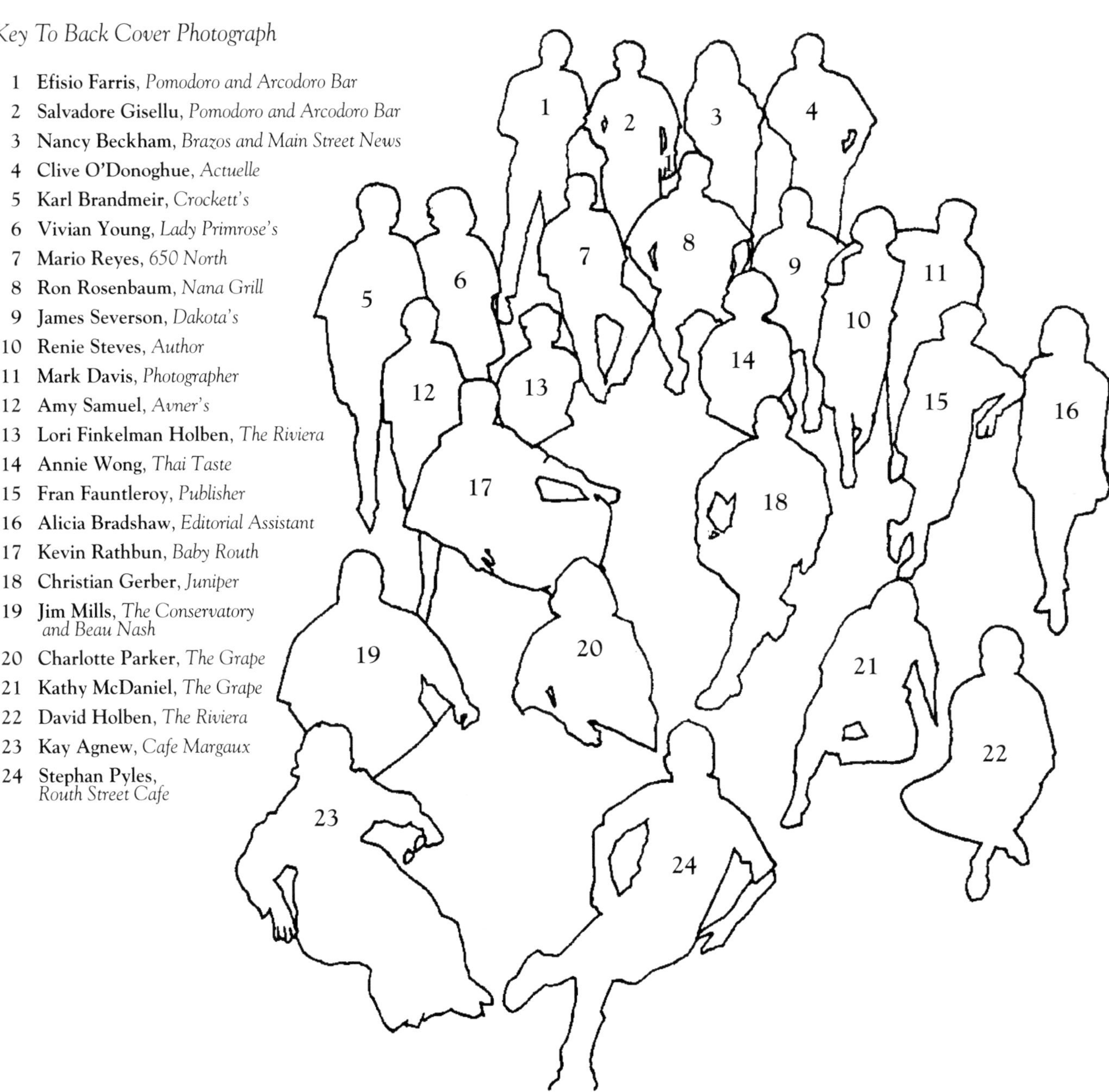

Dallas Is Cooking!
ORDER FORM

Name

Address

City State Zip

Telephone

My check or money order is enclosed.

✔	Quantity	Price	Shipping	Total
	1 Copy	$15.95	$2.00*	**$17.95**
	2 Copies	$31.90	$4.00*	**$35.90**
	3 Copies	$47.85	$6.00*	**$53.85**

*Make checks payable to
Dallas Is Cooking! and mail to:*

DALLAS IS COOKING!
1406 Thomas Place
Fort Worth, Texas 76107-2432

** Texas residents please add $1.24 (7.75%) per copy for sales tax.*

Wholesale orders are welcome! Qualified buyers please contact Fran Fauntleroy at 713/621-3230 to place an order.

Dallas Is Cooking!
ORDER FORM

Name

Address

City State Zip

Telephone

My check or money order is enclosed.

✔	Quantity	Price	Shipping	Total
	1 Copy	$15.95	$2.00*	**$17.95**
	2 Copies	$31.90	$4.00*	**$35.90**
	3 Copies	$47.85	$6.00*	**$53.85**

*Make checks payable to
Dallas Is Cooking! and mail to:*

DALLAS IS COOKING!
1406 Thomas Place
Fort Worth, Texas 76107-2432

** Texas residents please add $1.24 (7.75%) per copy for sales tax.*

Wholesale orders are welcome! Qualified buyers please contact Fran Fauntleroy at 713/621-3230 to place an order.